Handspan of Red Earth

Handspan of Red Earth

An Anthology of American Farm Poems

Edited by Catherine Lewallen Marconi

University of Iowa Press Ψ Iowa City

University of Iowa Press,
Iowa City 52242
Copyright © 1991 by
the University of Iowa
All rights reserved
Printed in the United
States of America
Second printing, 1991

Design by Richard Hendel

Printed on acid-free paper

The Grant Wood lithographs are
reproduced courtesy of the University
of Iowa Museum of Art.
Page iii: *Approaching Storm,* 1940
Page 1: *Sultry Night,* 1939
Page 45: *March,* 1939
Page 85: *February,* 1940
Page 133: *July Fifteenth,* 1938

Library of Congress
Cataloging-in-Publication Data
Handspan of red earth: an anthology
    of American farm poems/edited by
    Catherine Lewallen Marconi.—1st ed.
        p.   cm.
    ISBN 0-87745-325-X (alk. paper),
ISBN 0-87745-326-8 (pbk.: alk. paper)
    1. Farm life—Poetry. 2. American
poetry. I. Marconi, Catherine
Lewallen, 1944–
PS595.F38H36   1991   90-21163
811′.54080355—dc20   CIP

To the memory of

John Lindley Lewallen (1897 – 1989)

and to my mother,

Alberta Webster Lewallen

I lay close to the dirt and looked through fenestrated

   wheat.

A white star froze the focus of my gaze.

Its straight beam called a terror to my heart.

The love, it said, the love you have of dirt

Rots out pure images and forms all symbolism into a

   moulded peat.

   —Alberta Webster, 1939

Contents

II. Stretching Fence Wire

III. Shanks, Sawgrass

IV. Open Furrows

Acknowledgments

It has been my pleasure to collect these poems about our contemporary American farms. To the following friends who helped make this book possible: Dennis Schmitz, William Stafford, Roger Weingarten, Catherine French, Gary Short, John Anton Pillar, Denise Lichtig, Dianna Henning, Lisa Shannon, Mary Madsen, and Kim Silveira-Wolterbeek; to the financial supporters who helped pay the permissions fees to reprint the poems: Bank of America, Stockton Savings and Loan, Farmers and Merchants Bank, and Raj Bisla; and to my children, Sarah and Matthew, for their ongoing support—thank you.

Preface

On my morning mail run, that five or so miles from my home
on Clements Road to Linden (pop. 2,300 +), I drive from
these low, rolling Sierra Nevada foothills south to delicate
bottomland of wyman silt loam and sandy loam—some of the
world's most fertile and productive farmland. Clements Road
dead-ends on Comstock Road, and if I were to gear my Jeep
down and head right out cross-country, I'd drive through
prime farmland, hundred-acre family farms and orchards.
I'd drive through one of America's largest walnut orchards.
In fact, any road I'd take to Linden would pass kidney bean
fields, tomato fields, peach, almond, pear, cherry, and apple
orchards—Granny Smith, Golden Delicious, Mutsu, Royal
Gala, and Fuji apples.

When I drive west, toward Stockton (pop. 220,000 +),
along Comstock Road, then turn north onto Duncan, I pass
orchards that flow into onion fields, alfalfa fields, 160-acre
blocks of field corn, and finally, at the first major intersec-
tion, at Eight Mile Road and Highway 99, I slow down, stop.
Even wait. A dust cloud boils up from the Caterpillar D-10
hauling an earthmover, from backhoes, truckloads of con-
duit, and the Cat-yellow road grader whose fifteen-foot
steel blade is skimming the red loam. And, of course, out in
the field, the ever-present building contractor, hard hat
pushed back, is bent over blueprints for another 155-acre
subdivision on San Joaquin Valley soil.

This morning, while standing in the check-out line at Bi-
Rite (one of Linden's three family-owned and -operated
grocery stores), I listened to a familiar conversation. The
new truck driver for Pepsi-Cola was scoping the Linden
area for a home to buy. As I fixed my gaze on his blue

shirt—its red-white-and blue Pepsi emblem blurring—my mind flashed on Crèvecoeur's *Letters from an American Farmer*, written between 1769 and 1782. Just two days ago I'd read letter 2, "On the Situation, Feelings, and Pleasures, of an American Farmer," in which Crèvecoeur wrote: "The instant I enter on my own land, the bright idea of property, of exclusive right, of independence, exalt my mind. Precious soil, I say to myself, by what singular custom of law is it that thou wast made to constitute the riches of the freeholder? What should we American farmers be without the distinct possession of that soil?"

And, still seeing that blurred Pepsi emblem, I flashed on Thoreau living on Emerson's property from 1845 to 1847, a time when he allowed his imagination to buy farms from his neighbors, then plow, seed, and harvest the rich loam near Concord. Of that farm ground Thoreau wrote, in *Walden*: "I have frequently seen a poet withdraw, having enjoyed the most valuable part of a farm, while the crusty farmer supposed that he had got a few wild apples only. Why, the owner does not know it for many years when a poet has put his farm in rhyme, the most admirable kind of invisible fence, has fairly impounded it, milked it, skimmed it, and got all the cream, and left the farmer only the skimmed milk."

Today's American poets, still enjoying "the most valuable part of a farm," have separated the cream from the farms for their poems. From the bean fields and vineyards of California's San Joaquin Valley to the hog farms of Iowa's Henry County, from the cattle ranches of Nevada sage land to the number 2 yellow corn fields of the Heartland, from the wheat fields of the Dakotas to the apple orchards of Freedom, New Hampshire, poets continue stretching invisible fence wire in their poems, creating from the sharp emotions and details of this shared farm poem an inspiring reverence.

The poets in this anthology have in common a farming background or an absorbing interest in farm life. The poems were selected for their distinct diversity and sensitivity to farm life. Each poem in the collection is an apple picked from the barrel because it provides another sustaining image of the contemporary American farm.

I. Sharecroppers

A Human Condition

If there is a forest anywhere
the one you live with whimpers in her
sleep or construes a glance wrong, awake:
without intent she falls toward zero
impact; like an indicator on a chart
she rounds into terror, and the wild trees
try for her throat,
    if there is a forest anywhere.

If you concur with a world that has forests
in it, the one you live with will indict
you. If you like a farm, it will threaten.
Some people casually help each other:
if one likes a place the other finds
a kind going out of the breath at evening there.
    At your house any forest is everywhere.

But there are farms—to see them in the evening
extends your breath; you hover their hills
with regard for a world that offers human beings
a lavish, a deepening abode, in the evening,
like them. These places could have been home,
are lost to you now. They are foreign but good.
    There are these farms.

WILLIAM STAFFORD

When I Was Young

That good river that flowed backward
when it felt the danger of Babylon
taught the rest of us in the story how to be good,
but my mother said, "God, I used to love that town."

Animals that knew the way to Heaven
wagged at the back doors of every house
when I was young, and horses told fences
the story of Black Beauty, and smelled of the good manger.

Those times tested the pre-war clocks, and
cold mornings they rang and rang. I haven't recently
seen rivers flow backward or animals that remember.
The clocks, though, still pursue what they endlessly loved.

WILLIAM STAFFORD

Eclogues

where I lived the river
    lay like a blue wrist
between the bluffs & the islands
were tiny unctions of green. where
    every morning the horses outside
my house woke the sun & their breath
was like wet foliage
    in the cool air. but in my house
my bedroom poised
    between shadow & light & the light
was flawed by angles of glass
till night disappeared in a moment
    of wonder. the farm fed
on the full hillsides & sheets
of grain seemed to fall
    almost to the river's shore.
but from my window the farm
    was less real: the river & at noon
the fish I could almost hear fading
in its cool depths distracted
    the boy of twelve. my brother
beside me
    slept. he was oldest & duty
has deliberate solitude: even my sisters
kept their dolls
    quietly.

the second son: his father
is silent. whose hands are fouled
    with the birth of a new foal & the brother
fixes the blanket

over the mare's belly. the blood! & the younger
        boy thinks the flesh
a burden & at fault
        for its own pain. the others
lift the foal & pull
the small genital till it flexes
with full life.
        I stood in the barn
born second of God's beasts
        & alone in the days of my making.

my grandfather's God
guided him to the river & the Holy
        Ghost, he said, hung
like a white hand over this hill. our farm
        was his & when he died
my father (his son) worked a stone
in the shape of a bird, wings
        upraised as if startled
by my grandfather's death.

my name came from the river
the Fox called "Father" &
        "Source" as if a man's semen
were the only cause & my mother's fluid
        a mere aspiration. my mother
told of monsters who may
have died in the river-bed & she read
        that ice a mile high once
moved over their bones. at night
        the river with cold friction

pushes my slumbering flesh
      & my manhood moves
new
& in its own seed.

my father
      died, feeder of many horses & so fine
an ear he had
he heard the birds with feathered weight
      drop between the green rows
of corn. a gothic
man knowing
no wisdom & in that field we
      no longer plant. the birds
forever float
      above his grave & the ground
gives
more each year.

that winter the farm
      dozed, its tillage deep
in snow. the river
backs a cruel spine against
      the bluffs & boyhood's
dim fish ride
up under the ice, Mother:
      your children. inside
the fire rubs
itself for warmth & the windows
go white with frost.

DENNIS SCHMITZ

Freedom, New Hampshire

1

We came to visit the cow
Dying of fever,
Towle said it was already
Shovelled under, in a secret
Burial-place in the woods.
We prowled through the woods
Weeks, we never

Found where. Other
Kids other summers
Must have found the place
And asked, Why is it
Green here? The rich
Guess a grave, maybe,
The poor think a pit

For dung, like the one
We shovelled in in the fall
That came up green
The next year, that may as well
Have been the grave
Of a cow or something
For all that shows. A kid guesses
By whether his house has a bathroom.

2

We found a cowskull once; we thought it was
From one of the asses in the Bible, for the sun

Shone into the holes through which it had seen
Earth as an endless belt carrying gravel, had heard
Its truculence cursed, had learned how sweat
Stinks, and had brayed—shone into the holes
With solemn and majestic light, as if some
Skull somewhere could be Baalbek or the Parthenon.

That night passing Towle's Barn
We saw lights. Towle had lassoed a calf
By its hind legs, and he tugged against the grip
Of the darkness. The cow stood by chewing millet.
Derry and I took hold, too, and hauled.
It was sopping with darkness when it came free.
It was a bullcalf. The cow mopped it awhile,
And we walked around it with a lantern,

And it was sunburned, somehow, and beautiful.
It took a dug as the first business
And sneezed and drank at the milk of light.
When we got it balanced on its legs, it went wobbling
Towards the night. Walking home in darkness
We saw the July moon looking on Freedom, New
    Hampshire,
We smelled the fall in the air, it was the summer,
We thought, Oh this is but the summer!

3

Once I saw the moon
Drift into the sky like a bright
Pregnancy pared

From a goddess who thought
To be beautiful she must keep slender—
Cut loose, and drifting up there
To happen by itself—
And waning, in lost labor;

As we lost our labor
Too—afternoons
When we sat on the gate
By the pasture, under the Ledge,
Buzzing and skirling on toilet-
papered combs tunes
To the rumble-seated cars
Taking the Ossipee Road

On Sundays; for
Though dusk would come upon us
Where we sat, and though we had
Skirled out our hearts in the music,
Yet the dandruffed
Harps we skirled it on
Had done not much better than
Flies, which buzzed, when quick

We trapped them in our hands,
Which went silent when we
Crushed them, which we bore
Downhill to the meadowlark's
Nest full of throats
Which Derry charmed and combed
With an Arabian air, while I
Chucked crushed flies into

Innards I could not see,
For the night had fallen
And the crickets shrilled on all sides
In waves, as if the grassleaves
Shrieked by hillsides
As they grew, and the stars
Made small flashes in the sky,
Like mica flashing in rocks

On the chokecherried Ledge
Where bees I stepped on once
Hit us from behind like a shotgun,
And where we could see
Windowpanes in Freedom flash
And Loon Lake and Winnipesaukee
Flash in the sun
And the blue world flashing.

4

The fingerprints of our eyeballs would zigzag
On the sky; the clouds that came drifting up
Our fingernails would drift into the thin air;
In bed at night there was music if you listened,
Of an old surf breaking far away in the blood.

Kids who come by chance on grass green for a man
Can guess cow, dung, man, anything they want,
To them it is the same. To us who knew him as he was
After the beginning and before the end, it is green
For a name called out of the confusions of the earth—

11

Winnipesaukee coined like a moon, a bullcalf
Dragged from the darkness where it breaks up again,
Larks which long since have crashed for good in the grass
To which we fed the flies, buzzing ourselves like flies,
While the crickets shrilled beyond us, in July . . .

The mind may sort it out and give it names—
When a man dies he dies trying to say without slurring
The abruptly decaying sounds. It is true
That only flesh dies, and spirit flowers without stop
For men, cows, dung, for all dead things; and it is good,
    yes—

But an incarnation is in particular flesh
And the dust that is swirled into a shape
And crumbles and is swirled again had but one shape
That was this man. When he is dead the grass
Heals what he suffered, but he remains dead,
And the few who loved him know this until they die.

For my brother, 1925–1957

GALWAY KINNELL

Farmer's Daughter

There's always unseasonable weather.
Remember the flood that killed father:
when the water went down, the chickens
lay muddy and drowned. Oh we watch
the weather here on earth; we don't forget
the winter days when girls wear cotton dresses,
the Aprils when the bushes sag with snow.
      We were cutting the apple trees back
      when he said, "Look, it's snowing";
      but I'd seen a winter of snow
      and knew that more were coming.
Still, what do we know of a season?
Only father could say
when the rain would stop at the mountain
or ruin the hay. I'd try to watch
the hawks or lick a finger,
and the crops were still a failure;
there was frost all over the valley,
south as far as Twin Falls.
      He kissed me when shadows were long
      on the path to the orchard; he promised
      to meet me again when the apples were in;
now when the wind parts the curtains,
now in the city when the cat won't come,
I sleep with only one eye shut,
keeping a weather eye out.

ANNIE DILLARD

13

The Farm on the Great Plains

A telephone line goes cold;
birds tread it wherever it goes.
A farm back of a great plain
tugs an end of the line.

I call that farm every year,
ringing it, listening, still;
no one is home at the farm,
the line gives only a hum.

Some year I will ring the line
on a night at last the right one,
and with an eye tapered for braille
from the phone on the wall

I will see the tenant who waits—
the last one left at the place;
through the dark my braille eye
will lovingly touch his face.

"Hello, is Mother at home?"
No one is home today.
"But Father—he should be there."
No one—no one is here.

"But you—are you the one . . . ?"
Then the line will be gone
because both ends will be home:
no space, no birds, no farm.

My self will be the plain,
wise as winter is gray,
pure as cold posts go
pacing toward what I know.

WILLIAM STAFFORD

The Man Who Buys Hides

before I had a face
my mother supposed another horizon
aligned with that

wrong one contemporary hands fit
to relic Sioux.
maybe town behind the long
hills her brother's feedlot rode.
she was unmarried & wished

my face would never ripen
on the small stone memory left
of a necessary
lover. but I was born

white. & grew, bulky
& slow, never hearing my name
knotted in her tongue though
she must have sung

kneading father's pale
flesh, face to face drinking
distortion from each ripple
the other's body made.
or so I thought
when at night her lost
voice sounded the walls to the service
porch where at fourteen I dreamed
one pool dropping

to another hatchery trout threaded.
on the wall overhead

an exhausted
Jesus dried in milky shellac,

showing rain.
             *   *   *
summers I answered
her face surfacing in the bedroom
window to clean her eyes

or devotedly follow a crippled
hand through the word
"drink." my denim printed
blue sweat wherever I leaned
in her unquenchable

shadow. winters the ragged sky
my eyes folded as I slept
lost snow. the world formed under

our stamping feet & above it
breath drifted. with bare
hands uncle & I
shaped the cattle's frozen
noses, undid the ice their drool
tied through whatever
they ate. only the radio

spoke other names
when the lights were out
& eyes were adrift in their own

local winter.

       *   *   *

forty years later never thinking
of Dakota I still go faceless
into sleep & dream myself

intaglio under the animal.
I never see the driver
of my truck as it weaves the dead
smells through eucalyptus rows
swerving for potholes

in the gravel till the bones
give & under the tarp
the burst organs suck & squeeze.
what is death?
at the tail end they put one drain
at the other end they put
the tongue back in, intractable
& too big—
what can the doctor say

who is tired of his own body?

       *   *   *

the poplar leaves go on multiplying
basic July. July sun
is swollen in the basin

where I cool
my drunken face. once I loved
my smell as I loved the hoof tipped
with stink trailing from the stud

barn. I have become a talker
in bars who wanted
to be only a handspan of red
earth trembling with ants.
Dakota stays under the washed
face even if Calif
turns it dark. only man is dumb

whose tongue shapes before the fingers
know. did these dead
animals talk

with hooves or with tactile
fetlocks praise
the grass as they stepped

off the limits of their hunger,
touching with their mouths
last? as I load each distended

body the winch
squeals, the cable cuts new
boundaries across
a piebald hide. only the head
drags & the eyes roll

over, counter to the earth.

DENNIS SCHMITZ

The Sheep Child

Farm boys wild to couple
With anything   with soft-wooded trees
With mounds of earth   mounds
Of pinestraw   will keep themselves off
Animals by legends of their own:
In the hay-tunnel dark
And dung of barns, they will
Say   I have heard tell

That in a museum in Atlanta
Way back in a corner somewhere
There's this thing that's only half
Sheep   like a woolly baby
Pickled in alcohol   because
Those things can't live   his eyes
Are open   but you can't stand to look
I heard from somebody who . . .

But this is now almost all
Gone. The boys have taken
Their own true wives in the city,
The sheep are safe in the west hill
Pasture   but we who were born there
Still are not sure. Are we,
Because we remember, remembered
In the terrible dust of museums?

Merely with his eyes, the sheep-child may

Be saying   saying

I am here, in my father's house.
I who am half of your world, came deeply
To my mother in the long grass
Of the west pasture, where she stood like moonlight
Listening for foxes. It was something like love
From another world that seized her
From behind, and she gave, not lifting her head
Out of dew, without ever looking, her best
Self to that great need. Turned loose, she dipped
  her face
Farther into the chill of the earth, and in a sound
Of sobbing   of something stumbling
Away, began, as she must do,
To carry me. I woke, dying,

In the summer sun of the hillside, with my eyes
Far more than human. I saw for a blazing moment
The great grassy world from both sides,
Man and beast in the round of their need,
And the hill wind stirred in my wool,
My hoof and my hand clasped each other,
I ate my one meal
Of milk, and died
Staring. From dark grass I came straight

To my father's house, whose dust
Whirls up in the halls for no reason
When no one comes   piling deep in a hellish
  mild corner,
And, through my immortal waters,

I meet the sun's grains eye
To eye, and they fail at my closet of glass.
Dead, I am most surely living
In the minds of farm boys: I am he who drives
Them like wolves from the hound bitch and calf
And from the chaste ewe in the wind.
They go into woods   into bean fields   they go
Deep into their known right hands. Dreaming of
*   me,*
They groan   they wait   they suffer
Themselves, they marry, they raise their kind.

JAMES DICKEY

Maple Syrup

August, goldenrod blowing. We walk
into the graveyard, to find
my grandfather's grave. Ten years ago
I came here last, bringing
marigolds from the round garden
outside the kitchen.
I didn't know you then.
                        We walk
among carved names that go with photographs
on top of the piano at the farm:
Keneston, Wells, Fowler, Batchelder, Buck.
We pause at the new grave
of Grace Fenton, my grandfather's
sister. Last summer
we called on her at the nursing home,
eighty-seven, and nodding
in a blue housedress. We cannot find
my grandfather's grave.
                        Back at the house
where no one lives, we potter
and explore the back chamber
where everything comes to rest: spinning wheels,
pretty boxes, quilts,
bottles, books, albums of postcards.
Then with a flashlight we descend
firm steps to the root cellar—black,
cobwebby, huge,
with dirt floors and fieldstone walls,
and above the walls, holding the hewn
sills of the house, enormous
granite foundation stones.

Past the empty bins
for squash, apples, carrots, and potatoes,
we discover the shelves for canning, a few
pale pints
of tomato left, and—what
is this?—syrup, maple syrup
in a quart jar, syrup
my grandfather made twenty-five
years ago
for the last time.
                    I remember
coming to the farm in March
in sugaring time, as a small boy.
He carried the pails of sap, sixteen-quart
buckets, dangling from each end
of a wooden yoke
that lay across his shoulders, and emptied them
into a vat in the saphouse
where fire burned day and night
for a week.
                    Now the saphouse
tilts, nearly to the ground,
like someone exhausted
to the point of death, and next winter
when snow piles three feet thick

on the roofs of the cold farm,
the saphouse will shudder and slide
with the snow to the ground.
                    Today
we take my grandfather's last

quart of syrup
upstairs, holding it gingerly,
and we wash off twenty-five years
of dirt, and we pull
and pry the lid up, cutting the stiff,
dried rubber gasket, and dip our fingers
in, you and I both, and taste
the sweetness, you for the first time,
the sweetness preserved, of a dead man
in his own kitchen,
giving us
from his lost grave the gift of sweetness.

DONALD HALL

How to Make Rhubarb Wine

Go to the patch some afternoon
in early summer, fuzzy with beer
and sunlight, and pick a sack
of rhubarb (red or green will do)
and God knows watch for rattlesnakes
or better, listen; they make a sound
like an old lawn mower rolled downhill.
Wear a hat. A straw hat's best
for the heat but lets the gnats in.
Bunch up the stalks and chop the leaves off
with a buck knife and be careful.
You need ten pounds; a grocery bag
packed full will do it. Then go home
and sit barefooted in the shade
behind the house with a can of beer.
Spread out the rhubarb in the grass
and wash it with cold water
from the garden hose, washing
your feet as well. Then take a nap.
That evening, dice the rhubarb up
and put it in a crock. Then pour
eight quarts of boiling water in,
cover it up with a checkered cloth
to keep the fruit flies out of it,
and let it stand five days or so.
Take time each day to think of it.

Ferment ten days, under the cloth,
sniffing of it from time to time,
then siphon it off, swallowing some,

and bottle it. Sit back and watch
the liquid clear to honey yellow,
bottled and ready for the years,
and smile. You've done it awfully well.

TED KOOSER

The Wife

He leaves her on the farm, where doors don't lock,
and takes the household pistol on his rounds.
She stands for twenty years across the field
and breathes his dust. At night he tries to stroke
her hair: she stiffens up. His hand lies cracked
behind his knee. Yet when the gin forecloses
his tab, or Tony's Chinese Market calls,
she soaks the beans like always, and understands
that loving him means knowing that her chance
to ripen whole is small. She wanders back
into the burnt and puny cotton, sags against
the palo verde's trunk. The branches
rattle, full of pods. Her boots leave streaks
in mud as she crams white bolls in gunny sacks.

PEGGY SHUMAKER

The Orchard

We go into it at night.
In Wyoming an orchard is the
only city around—so many blossoms going up
into trees like lights
and windfall apples like lives
coming down.

In the pickup, heads on the tailgate,
we lie on last year's hay and wait
for the orchard to bloom.

A great horned owl sweeps between
trees as if to cropdust the rising
sap with white for the flowers.

"The first blossom to come," you say,
"I'll give the apple that grows there to you."

Another owl lands
on a bare branch and drops
a plug of micebones to the roots.
Under him, the tree does not think of
the sap's struggle.
I listen to your heart. Divided by
beats and rests, it says yes, then no, then yes.

Above us the Milky Way seams the sky and is
stirred by a hand too big to see.
We watch the stars.

Tonight so many of them fall.

GRETEL EHRLICH

The Tenant Farmer

Hailstones puncture the ground,
as I sit at the table, rubbing a fork.
My woman slides a knife across her lips,
then lays it beside a cup of water.
Each day she bites another notch in her thumb
and I pretend relief is coming
as the smooth black tire, Earth,
wheels around the sun without its patch of topsoil,
and my mouth speaks: *wheat, barley, red cabbage,*
roll on home to Jesus,
it's too late now you're dead.

A I

The Country Midwife: A Day

I bend over the woman.
This is the third time between abortions.
I dip a towel into a bucket of hot water
and catch the first bit of blood,
as the blue-pink dome of a head breaks through.
A scraggy, red child comes out of her into my hands
like warehouse ice sliding down the chute.

It's done, the stink of birth, Old Grizzly
rears up on his hind legs in front of me
and I want to go outside,
but the air smells the same there too.
The woman's left eye twitches
and beneath her, a stain as orange as sunrise
spreads over the sheet.
I lift my short, blunt fingers to my face
and I let her bleed, Lord, I let her bleed.

A I

Young Farm Woman Alone

What could I do with a man?—
pull him on like these oxhide boots,
the color of plums, dipped in blue ink
and stomp hell out of my loneliness,
this hoe that with each use grows sharper.

A I

Gretel

Don't say, "Who can understand
this life," and mean the oatmeal
or the whole milk
and butter it swims in
I was out walking this morning
after breakfast
in my rubber boots
with my old goat. Gretel
could still win best-of-show
just for showing up
and for the shape of her udder
Attachment *is* what you look for
in a goat
when you're judging
and we love our walk together
down to the creek
through the wet pasture
Light, everywhere, is an appointment
we should keep
when we are quiet
enough, and can find the path

TOM CRAWFORD

Gretel (II)

We are like two old miners
Gretel, you and I,
far from the world
working, as best we can, this claim
we have on each other
For the poet and his goat
no day is ordinary
the way we love to eat
our way through
what light has given
The branch of sweet elderberry
you can't reach
I pull down
It's that kind of relationship
when words mean less
than leaves
which your long, black tongue
curls around, another morning
we don't pay Caesar's taxes
Nothing lost then—what color is
to invention
A red plane scoots over the trees
now, and disappears

TOM CRAWFORD

34

A Sheeprancher Named John

A swarming.
Orange as bees into hair, a face.
In a long overcoat of them he moves swiftly
by stings and grace across Big Horn Mountains
against an upstream current of sheep.
When he speaks it is brutally to the point.
His fingers taper. A diamond ring orbits one of them
and is glazed by the silkdust of oats.
Orange, not direct light but
slanted, helplessly elegant, a color of
minor disrepute—faded chiffon draped
on the high, startled bones of his face.
Skin crisscrossed, uncertain tracks of aging,
irregular hems sewn, the threads pulled out.
His whole body, orange and burnt orange.
The abalone shell of his back with rich meat
under it, perfectly plumbed and moving sideways in
the sign of Cancer.
On his arms, sunspots like birdseed melted and
scraped smooth—burns on powdery skin.
How could it be so soft in a climate that weathers?
Mouth, a loose tear across the face, rarely
moved by shapes of words, but a listening apparatus—
lips slide apart, mark feelings awash and received.
Eyes are steady-state. Burnt all the way brown.
Shy penis, mostly
swirled white.

GRETEL EHRLICH

Picking Grapes in an Abandoned Vineyard

Picking grapes alone in the late autumn sun—
A short, curved knife in my hand,
Its blade silver from so many sharpenings,
Its handle black.
I still have a scar where a friend
Sliced open my right index finger, once,
In a cutting shed—
The same kind of knife.
The grapes drop into the pan,
And the gnats swarm over them, as always.
Fifteen years ago,
I worked this row of vines beside a dozen
Families up from Mexico.
No one spoke English, or wanted to.
One woman, who made an omelet with a sheet of tin
And five, light blue quail eggs,
Had a voice full of dusk, and jail cells,
And bird calls. She spoke,
In Spanish, to no one, as they all did.
Their swearing was specific,
And polite.
I remember two of them clearly:
A man named Tea, six feet, nine inches tall
At the age of sixty-two,
Who wore white spats into downtown Fresno
Each Saturday night,
An alcoholic giant whom the women loved—
One chilled morning, they found him dead outside
The Rose Café . . .
And Angel Domínguez,
Who came to work for my grandfather in 1910,

And who saved for years to buy
Twenty acres of rotting, Thompson Seedless vines.
While the sun flared all one August,
He decided he was dying of a rare disease,
And spent his money and his last years
On specialists,
Who found nothing wrong.
Tea laughed, and, tipping back
A bottle of Muscatel, said: "Nothing's wrong.
You're just dying."
At seventeen, I discovered
Parlier, California, with its sad, topless bar,
And its one main street, and its opium.
I would stand still, and chalk my cue stick
In Johnny Palores' East Front Pool Hall, and watch
The room filling with tobacco smoke, as the sun set
Through one window.
Now all I hear are the vines rustling as I go
From one to the next,
The long canes holding up dry leaves, reddening,
So late in the year.
What the vines want must be this silence spreading
Over each town, over the dance halls and the dying parks,
And the police drowsing in their cruisers
Under the stars.
What the men who worked here wanted was
A drink strong enough
To let out what laughter they had.
I can still see the two of them:
Tea smiles and lets his yellow teeth shine—
While Angel, the serious one, for whom

Death was a rare disease,
Purses his lips, and looks down, as if
He is already mourning himself—
A soft, gray hat between his hands.
Today, in honor of them,
I press my thumb against the flat part of this blade,
And steady a bunch of red, Málaga grapes
With one hand,
The way they showed me, and cut—
And close my eyes to hear them laugh at me again,
And then, hearing nothing, no one,
Carry the grapes up into the solemn house,
Where I was born.

LARRY LEVIS

Getting the Mail

I walk back
toward the frog pond, carrying
the one letter, a few wavy lines
crossing the stamp: tongue-streaks
from the glue
and spittle beneath: my sign.

The frogs'
eyes bulge toward the visible, suddenly
an alderfly glitters past, declining
to die: her third giant step
into the world.

And touching
the name stretched over the letter
like a blindfold, I wonder,
what did *getting warm* used to mean? And tear

open the words,
to the far-off, serene
groans of a cow
a farmer is milking in the August dusk
and the Kyrie of a chainsaw drifting down off Wheelock
    Mountain.

GALWAY KINNELL

From Letter to an Imaginary Friend

4

My father took me as far as he could that summer,
Those midnights, mostly, back from his long haul.
But mostly Cal, one of the bundle teamsters,
My sun-blackened Virgil of the spitting circle,
Led me from depth to depth.
                                        Toward the light
I was too young to enter.
He must have been about thirty. As thin as a post,
As tough as whang-leather, with a brick-topped mulish
    face,
A quiet talker. He read *The Industrial Worker*,
Though I didn't know what the paper was at the time.
The last of the real Wobs—that, too, I didn't know,
Couldn't.
                        Played a harmonica; sat after supper
In the lantern smell and late bat-whickering dusk,
Playing mumbly-peg and talked of wages and hours
At the bunkhouse door. On Sunday cleaned his gun,
A Colt .38 that he let me shoot at a hawk—
It jumped in my hand and my whole arm tingled with
    shock.
A quiet man with the smell of the road on him,
The smell of far places. Romantic as all of the stiffs
Were romantic to me and my cousins,
Stick-in-the-mud burgesses of boyhood's country.

What he tried to teach me was how to take my time,
Not to be impatient, not to shy at the fences,
Not to push on the reins, not to baulk nor pull leather.

Tried to teach me when to laugh and when to be serious,
When to laugh at the serious, be serious in my laughter,
To laugh at myself and be serious with myself.
He wanted me to grow without growing too fast for myself.
A good teacher, a brother.

5

That was the year, too, of the labor troubles on the rigs—
The first, or the last maybe. I heard the talk.
It was dull. Then, one day—windy—
We were threshing flax I remember, toward the end of the
     run—
After quarter-time I think—the slant light falling
Into the blackened stubble that shut like a fan toward the
     headland—
The strike started then. Why *then* I don't know.
Cal spoke for the men and my uncle cursed him.
I remember that ugly sound, like some animal cry touching
     me
Deep and cold, and I ran toward them
And the fighting started.
My uncle punched him. I heard the breaking crunch
Of his teeth going and the blood leaped out of his mouth
Over his neck and shirt—I heard their gruntings and
     strainings
Like love at night or men working hard together,
And heard the meaty thumpings, like beating a grain sack
As my uncle punched his body—I remember the dust
Jumped from his shirt.

He fell in the blackened stubble
Rose
Was smashed in the face
Stumbled up
Fell
Rose
Lay on his side in the harsh long slanting sun
And the blood ran out of his mouth and onto his shoulder.

Then I heard the quiet and that I was crying—
They had shut down the engine.
                              The last of the bundle-teams
Was coming in at a gallop.
                              Crying and cursing
Yelled at the crew: "Can't you jump the son-of-a-bitch!
Cal! Cal! get up"
But he didn't get up.
None of them moved.
Raging at my uncle I ran.
Got slapped,
Ran sobbing straight to the engine.
I don't know what I intended. To start the thing maybe,
To run her straight down the belt and into the feeder
Like a vast iron bundle.
I jammed the drive-lever over, lashed back on the throttle,
And the drive belt popped and jumped and the thresher
    groaned,
The beaters clutched at the air, knives flashed,
And I wrestled the clutch.
                              Far away, I heard them
Yelling my name, but it didn't sound like my own,

And the clutch stuck. (Did I want it to stick?) I hammered
    it
And the fireman came on a run and grabbed me and held
    me
Sobbing and screaming and fighting, my hand clenched
On the whistle rope while it screamed down all of our
    noises—
Stampeding a couple of empties into the field—
A long, long blast, hoarse, with the falling, brazen
Melancholy of engines when the pressure's falling.

Quiet then. My uncle was cursing the Reds,
Ordering the rig to start, but no one started.
The men drifted away.
                     The water monkey
Came in with his load.
                Questioned.
He got no answer.
Cal's buddy and someone else got him up
On an empty rack and they started out for home,
Him lying on the flat rack-bed.

Still crying, I picked up his hat that lay in the churned up
    dust,
And left my rack and team and my uncle's threats,
And cut for home across the river quarter.

THOMAS MCGRATH

II. Stretching Fence Wire

For the Hog Killing

Let them stand still for the bullet, and stare the shooter in
 the eye,
let them die while the sound of the shot is in the air, let
 them die as they fall,
let the jugular blood spring hot to the knife, let its freshet
 be full,
let this day begin again the change of hogs into people, not
 the other way around,
for today we celebrate again our lives' wedding with the
 world,
for by our hunger, by this provisioning, we renew the
 bond.

WENDELL BERRY

Prayers and Sayings of the Mad Farmer

I

It is presumptuous and irresponsible to pray for other people. A good man would pray only for himself—that he have as much good as he deserves, that he not receive more good or more evil than he deserves, that he bother nobody, that he not be bothered, that he want less. Praying thus for himself, he should prepare to live with the consequences.

II

> At night make me one with the darkness.
> In the morning make me one with the light.

III

If a man finds it necessary to eat garbage, he should resist the temptation to call it a delicacy.

IV

> Don't pray for the rain to stop.
> Pray for good luck fishing
> when the river floods.

V

Don't own so much clutter that you will be relieved to see
your house catch fire.

VI

Beware of the machinery of longevity. When a man's life is
over the decent thing is for him to die. The forest does not
withhold itself from death. What it gives up it takes back.

VII

Put your hands into the mire.
They will learn the kinship
of the shaped and the unshapen,
the living and the dead.

VIII

When I rise up
let me rise up joyful
like a bird.

When I fall
let me fall without regret
like a leaf.

IX

Sowing the seed,
my hand is one with the earth.

Wanting the seed to grow,
my mind is one with the light.

Hoeing the crop,
my hands are one with the rain.

Having cared for the plants,
my mind is one with the air.

Hungry and trusting,
my mind is one with the earth.

Eating the fruit,
my body is one with the earth.

X

Let my marriage be brought to the ground.
Let my love for this woman enrich the earth.

What is its happiness but preparing its place?
What is its monument but a rich field?

XI

By the excellence of his work the workman is a neighbor.
By selling only what he would not despise to own the
salesman is a neighbor. By selling what is good his
character survives his market.

XII

> Let me wake in the night
> and hear it raining
> and go back to sleep.

XIII

Don't worry and fret about the crops. After you have done
all you can for them, let them stand in the weather on
their own.

If the crop of any one year was all, a man would have to
cut his throat every time it hailed.

But the *real* products of any year's work are the farmer's
mind and the cropland itself.

If he raises a good crop at the cost of belittling himself and
diminishing the ground, he has gained nothing. He will
have to begin over again the next spring, worse off than
before.

Let him receive the season's increment into his mind. Let him work it into the soil.

The finest growth that farmland can produce is a careful farmer.

Make the human race a better head. Make the world a better piece of ground.

WENDELL BERRY

Fence Wire

Too tight, it is running over
Too much of this ground to be still
Or to do anything but tremble
And disappear left and right
As far as the eye can see

Over hills, through woods,
Down roads, to arrive at last
Again where it connects,
Coming back from the other side
Of animals, defining their earthly estate

As the grass becomes snow
While they are standing and dreaming
Of grass and snow.
The winter hawk that sits upon its post,
Feeling the airy current of the wires,

Turns into a robin, sees that this is wrong,
Then into a boy, and into a man who holds
His palm on the top tense strand
With the whole farm feeding slowly
And nervously into his hand.

If the wire were cut anywhere
All his blood would fall to the ground
And leave him standing and staring
With a face as white as a Hereford's.
From years of surrounding grain,

Cows, horses, machinery trying to turn
To rust, the humming arrives each second,
A sound that arranges these acres
And holds them highstrung and enthralled.
Because of the light, chilled hand

On the top thread tuned to an E
Like the low string of a guitar,
The dead corn is more
Balanced in death than it was,
The animals more aware

Within the huge human embrace
Held up and borne out of sight
Upon short, unbreakable poles
Wherethrough the ruled land intones
Like a psalm: properly,

With its eyes closed,
Whether on the side of the animals
Or not, whether disappearing
Right, left, through trees or down roads,
Whether outside, around, or in.

JAMES DICKEY

Male Image

I watch for my uncles to come in from the fields,
The three of them, big-shouldered men in overalls,
Their bare necks are streaked with dirt and sweat
Which I want to lick when they pick me up.
They are so warm and strong; they smell of summer:
The dark odor of horses, the dry green smell
Of tomato plants, the tan smell of loam.
They taste male and I can't get enough of that.

They also talk male. Everyone else calls me Teddy
Or Little Benny, after my father, who doesn't pick me up;
They call me "You *bondit*," which is Yiddish for rascal,
Or Butch McDevitt, which makes me feel like a cowboy.
When my uncle Moish puts Brownie in the stable,
He says, "Get in there, you son of a bitch."
Son of a bitch. I say it over and over after that,
When I rake the chicken yard, shuck the corn.
It's not a bad word anymore. Son of a bitch:
It's what men say when they are strong and happy
Because they have something hard to do.

TED SOLOTAROFF

The Snake

At the end of October
I found on the floor of the woods
a small snake whose back
was patterned with the dark
of the dead leaves he lay on.
His body was thickened with a mouse
or small bird. He was cold,
so stuporous with his full belly
and the fall air that he hardly
troubled to flicker his tongue.
I held him a long time, thinking
of the perfection of the dark
marking on his back, the death
that swelled him, his living cold.
Now the cold of him stays
in my hand, and I think of him
lying below the frost,
big with a death to nourish him
during a long sleep.

WENDELL BERRY

Trees and Cattle

Many trees can stand unshaded
In this place where the sun is alone,
But some may break out.
They may be taken to Heaven,
So gold is my only sight.

Through me, two red cows walk;
From a crowning glory
Of slowness they are not taken.
Let one hoof knock on a stone,
And off it a spark jump quickly,

And fire may sweep these fields,
And all outburn the blind sun.
Like a new light I enter my life,
And hover, not yet consumed,
With the trees in holy alliance,

About to be offered up,
About to get wings where we stand.
The whole field stammers with gold;
No leaf but is actively still;
There is no quiet or noise;

Continually out of a fire
A bull walks forth,
And makes of my mind a red beast
At each step feeling how
The sun more deeply is burning

Because trees and cattle exist.
I go away, in the end.
In the shade, my bull's horns die
From my head; in some earthly way
I have been given my heart:

Behind my back, a tree leaps up
On wings that could save me from death.
Its branches dance over my head.
Its flight strikes a root in me.
A cow beneath it lies down.

JAMES DICKEY

In the Upper Pasture

In the evergreen grove that abuts the pasture we are
limbing low branches, carting away deadwood,
cutting close to the trunk so the sap does not bleed,
to make a shelter, a run-in for foals and their mares.
We will not shorten the lives of these hemlocks and pines
in the afternoon of our lives, yet I am sad
to think that the dell will outlast us and our bloodlines.

Is this a pastoral? Be not deceived
by the bellows of leathery teats giving suck,
by the fringe of delicate beard that pricks
its braille notes on the muzzle of the newborn.
When instinct whinnies between dam and foal
at night in the rain, do not be lulled.
Each of us whimpers his way through the forest alone.

With scrap lumber we patiently fence off
a triad of trees that have grown so close to each other
a young horse darting through might be taken prisoner.
Let the babies be safe here, let them lie down on pine duff
away from the merciless blackflies, out of the weather.
Under the latticework of old trees let me stand
pitch-streaked and pleasured by this small thing we have
    done.

MAXINE KUMIN

In an Old Apple Orchard

The wind's an old man
to this orchard; these trees
have been feeling
the soft tug of his gloves
for a hundred years.
Now it's April again,
and again that old fool
thinks he's young.
He's combed the dead leaves
out of his beard; he's put on
perfume. He's gone off
late in the day
toward the town, and come back
slow in the morning,
reeling with bees.
As late as noon, if you look
in the long grass,
you can see him
still rolling about in his sleep.

TED KOOSER

Field Theory

In those days they grew sweet potatoes
big as newborn babies, and discovered
the power of clouds in boilers.
The spring said its diamonds under the poplars
and the spine twinkled like a milkyway.
Children shouted kickball and tag
from early evening until dark in the pasture.
I like to think they found in work
a soil subliminal and sublime.
Their best conspiracies were two
breathing in the night. They lived
on the upland atoll and didn't care
to step on horizons. And left no more
trace than a cloud shadow when I woke
from the coils of the cell's heart,
in the non-euclidean mountains,
recovering pieces of the morgenland.

ROBERT MORGAN

Hubcaps

The tractor runs over dirt and shapes it, turning
stubble and moving the hill
furrow by furrow to the terraces,
slicing clods, wearing
them away and chopping roots
to rot in sweet beds of decay.

The owl: eyes like arenas
gathering
the weeds and hungry ditches.
She guards the air like a monument
shedding a field of energy downwind.

Old hubcaps burning all night in the creek.

ROBERT MORGAN

Hay Scuttle

The holes in the floor of the barn loft
were cut for dropping shucks to the stalls.
Pile an armload on the opening
and stuff them through. The cow
is already eating as the rest
splash on her head. The fodder sweet
as tobacco is pushed down for the horse.
Light from below rises with manure
and warm cud-breath.
And bleach from the horse's bed.
Dark up here with the dead grass
and cornsheller, except for the trapdoors.
Only way out to the sun is down,
through the exquisite filth.

ROBERT MORGAN

Horses

When I was a boy here,
traveling the fields for pleasure,
the farms were worked with teams.
As late as then a teamster
was thought an accomplished man,
his art an essential discipline.
A boy learned it by delight
as he learned to use
his body, following the example
of men. The reins of a team
were put into my hands
when I thought the work was play.
And in the corrective gaze
of men now dead I learned
to flesh my will in power
great enough to kill me
should I let it turn.
I learned the other tongue
by which men spoke to beasts
—all its terms and tones.
And by the time I learned,
new ways had changed the time.
The tractors came. The horses
stood in the fields, keepsakes,
grew old, and died. Or were sold
as dogmeat. Our minds received
the revolution of engines, our will
stretched toward the numb endurance
of metal. And that old speech
by which we magnified

our flesh in other flesh
fell dead in our mouths.
The songs of the world died
in our ears as we went within
the uproar of the long syllable
of the motors. Our intent entered
the world as combustion.
Like our travels, our workdays
burned upon the world,
lifting its inwards up
in fire. Veiled in that power
our minds gave up the endless
cycle of growth and decay
and took the unreturning way,
the breathless distance of iron.

But that work, empowered by burning
the world's body, showed us
finally the world's limits
and our own. We had then
the life of a candle, no longer
the ever-returning song
among the grassblades and the leaves.

Did I never forget?
Or did I, after years,
remember? To hear that song
again, though brokenly
in the distances of memory,
is coming home. I came to

a farm, some of it unreachable
by machines, as some of the world
will always be. And so
I came to a team, a pair
of mares—sorrels, with white
tails and manes, beautiful!—
to keep my sloping fields.
Going behind them, the reins
tight over their backs as they stepped
their long strides, revived
again on my tongue the cries
of dead men in the living
fields. Now every move
answers what is still.
This work of love rhymes
living and dead. A dance
is what this plodding is.
A song, whatever is said.

WENDELL BERRY

At Nightfall

Like held lanterns, wavering,
almost gone out,
the cows' white faces turn towards me
as their bodies pivot, needles to magnetic north.
Squared off, they still, and stare.
I can barely make out the nostrils' dilation
trying to forage my scent from the currents of air,
or the draped-velvet black of their coats,
its crushed sheen.
As if all the brightness so recently glazing these hills
had gone into them when it went, had burnished
the heavy flanks with the gas-blue flame
whose low hiss is the letting down milk, or had opened
the dewlaps' deep curtains and stepped in behind,
drawing closed the body's opacity after.
Though some small part escapes still,
leaking through as we stand in mutual regard:
two cows, two calves, and a two-legged—
homelier animal, if truth be spoken, even than they.
Each of us pinned on the axis that spins out this dusk
as a pupa spins out her cocoon, white as the coming-in fog
being spun just now by the sea, or the milk spooling down
its long thread into udders
that guard the passage from all other lifetimes to this.
In the true north, that no iron points to,
the first stars scratch into the compass-glass of the sky.
One calf, grown restless, and pleased enough with this
    world,
butts the side of his dam; she shifts a little,
addresses me gravely a final question, then moves away,
right, I know, not to trust either me or my kind.

Then the fog reaches this place at the moment of darkness
and even the stars go out,
recede to the unfenced field of the no longer seen.
There, an assembly greets them:
the man, met once for an hour, who gave me the book he
    was reading;
the wooden recorder sighed into until I was ten,
tucked safely back in its sock of brown felt;
the seven lost watches, three rings, and near them the
    rhinestone pin
picked out for a teacher truly loved—
all the hard discarded and easily lost, the gone to the
    pastures of gone.
In a shadowy line, the cows enter:
first cow, then calf, then second cow, then second calf,
each broad nose following closely each knotted-rope tail.
They pause and gaze, seem content, then lower their
    heads
to the grass that rises from under the twinned quarter-
    moons of their hooves.
The grass grows green and greener: it is full daylight,
the air become warm, and filled with the cloverleaf-traffic
    of flies.
And though a dog is barking—
the white one, waving the plume of her tail—
the cows do not startle, beyond that now as they are,
so the barking continues, gaily, for a long time,
though growing more faint as I make my way up the side
    of the hill,
taking the path by foot-feel, leaving the low fog behind,
until suddenly from this side another dog answers,

equally happy but this one freckled, half-black, half-white,
with a tobacco-twist of color behind each ear,
answers and comes through the darkness, silencing
   crickets,
wagging me home, urging me   *faster, forward,*
into the impatient present, its spoked-wheel turnings,
wobblings, desires, where I—she seems quite sure of
   it—belong.

JANE HIRSHFIELD

Some Ashes Drifting above
Piedra, California

There is still one field I can love;
There is still a little darkness in each furrow
And each stump.
Behind it
You can sit down and begin to doubt
Even the hair on the backs of your hands—
And what you see now is nothing:
It is only
The scrubbed, wooden sink inside this shack
Abandoned by farm workers,
Or, above a kitchen window, only a strip of curtain
Which is the color of no flag
And no country, though once it meant *night*—
And so the occupant stared out at the sky whitening
Into each dawn—
At all the withheld information
Which is sky,
And thought if he worked all day to shovel
Thirty acres of vines
Without once looking up into those torn clouds,
If he could sweat past such insolence into nightfall,
And ignore that, too, until he saw her
Turning from a bath,
Her skin suddenly
There, and darker than he could have believed—
As if night had entered the dusk
Of her body . . .
So their eyes and mouths opened, then.

And now,
If we listen for their laughter,

Which vanished fifteen years ago
Into the cleft wood of these boards,
Into the night and the rain,
It will sound like cold jewels spilling together,
It will sound like snow . . .
We will never have any money, either,
And we will go on staring past the sink,
Past the curtain,
And into a field which is not even white anymore,
Not even an orchard,
But simply this mud,
And always,
Over that, a hard sky.
And what I have to tell you now is only
The salt that ripens in our passing, and
Overwhelms us:
How I heard, once,
Of two lovers, who
Naked, and for a joke,
Tied themselves together with cast off clothes
And leaped into a canal—
Where the current held them under a whole hour.
I thought, then,
How each of them must have said all that can
Be said
Between a man and a woman—
As they fought each other to breathe,
Or, which is the same thing,
To be whole, and lonely again.
But I was wrong:
They only stiffened, and there were no words left

Inside them—
The man lay face down in the stillness;
The woman faced the sky.
Bobbing in the thick grass beside the banks,
Their arms whitened around each other for three days
In the stale water ...
Now they are these words.
And now, if I strike a match
To offer you
This page burned all the way
Into their silences,
Take it—
While your hair dies a little more
Into the day,
While the sun rises,
These two will be ashes in the palm of my hand,
Stirring a little and about to drift
Easily away, without comment,
On the wind.

LARRY LEVIS

Landscape in Spring

In a pickup my brother and me,
And some fat guy, are drinking from paper bags,
Our necks blackened, our hair loose in wind.
We're two thousand years from Jesus
And the foothills, saints, dogs running
In rain, Paris, women in Paris . . .
To the left, a Mexican waving us down with a hat.
To the right, a burst of tractor smoke
Coming apart, and a single house,
White and grumbling in the heat—
A woman in the yard with a hose pointed
At a tree. But we're not stopping,
And that house is going to stay
Where it is. We're speeding
Through the day, and if we're pointed
To a field, cotton or beet, we'll cut it
With a hoe. Good pay, bad pay,
It's all the same if you're brown
And given hours to think about the sun.
Work in dust, get up in dust. Beer makes it go.

GARY SOTO

73

A Place in Kansas

Somewhere in Kansas, a friend found
an empty stone house alone in a wheatfield.
Over the door was incised a ship's anchor.
There was no one to ask
what that anchor was doing in Kansas,
no water for miles.
Not a single white sail of a meaning
broke the horizon, though he stood there for hours.
It's like that in Kansas, forever.

TED KOOSER

In the Corners of Fields

Something is calling to me
from the corners of fields,
where the leftover fence wire
suns its loose coils, and stones
thrown out of the furrow
sleep in warm litters;
where the gray faces
of old No Hunting signs
mutter into the wind,
and dry horse tanks
spout fountains of sunflowers;
where a moth
flutters in from the pasture,
harried by sparrows,
and alights on a post,
so sure of its life
that it peacefully opens its wings.

TED KOOSER

Nebraska, Early March

The sun one hour from setting
distinguishes the landscape,
so red the barn,
so white the house,
each weathered board
so cleanly defined
on the slatted grainbin.
And the hay, each mound,
and the cattle, each calf
beside each cow so singular
against a slope of golden stubble,
and the stubble, each stalk,
and along the roadside the blue-
stem, each stem, and the fenceline,
each barb, and later the moon
through the window
washing our bodies, each
member, and your hair,
under my wildest touch each
indivisible strand.

WILLIAM KLOEFKORN

The Mad Farmer Shuts Himself inside His Silo to Sing Away the Storm

For and after Wendell Berry

Because the silo is round
each note is round,
each note eternity in a nutshell,
and knowing this the mad farmer
knows also that his song can never be lost,
never exhausted, never indefinitely contained,
that the notes will circle and circle
until the storm relents,
until the door left open permits them
freedom

and they will go then inevitable as seed
to the four great corners of the universe,
there to put themselves together over and over,
becoming over and over the song
that now at the height of the storm
the mad farmer hat in his hand
stands singing:

O la and la and earth and water and wind,
sunlight and shadow,
la and la and hands deep into the soil,
and work and love,
and the greatest of these is work
and love and hands, la and la and
the immaculate equation of knowhow
and concern

until the silo spins with the mad farmer's song,
until the storm with its thunder and lightning
joins in,
la and la and crack and rumble,
and knowing these, and the fathers
and the mothers and the children of these,
the mad farmer hat yet dripping in his hand
invents a final verse, releasing each word
with its attendant note whole as faith
into the space that waits to be more than itself
when the storm relents
and the sun does its own savage work
and the harvest behold! is in.

WILLIAM KLOEFKORN

Bows to Drouth

Driest summer,
The hose snakes under the mulch
   to the base of a gravenstein apple
   three years old,
And back to the standpipe
   Where it dives underground.

At the pump,
   the handle extended with pipe
   sweeps down
   six strokes to a gallon,
   one hundred and fifteen feet deep
   force pump, the cylinder sct in the water
Sucker-rod faintly clangs in the well.

Legs planted,
   both hands on the handle,
   whole body bending,
   I gaze through the trees and
   see different birds,
   different leaves,
   with each bow.

No counting,
   all free—
   deep water softly lifts out—
   over there—
At the base of an apple.

Drouth of the summer of '74

GARY SNYDER

79

Discovery

Plowing the nest of the lark
we breasted a sudden wave—
all the furrows in all the farms
and all the birds undisturbed.

There gleamed from where we came
one long continuous line—
fields where men had walked,
on many a nest of song.

WILLIAM STAFFORD

Grandfather

This would be before the war when sweet butter came
from a wooden churn and no one had heard of the word
cholesterol. The way in is past the old hay rake on the left,
the iron seat with its 26 holes (I counted them), is still
sound if I want to ride back to a field I could have sown
anywhere: Sweet Home . . . Chowchilla . . . USA. Red heads
of barley wave and rustle like a great sail in the afternoon
wind, rolling first one way, then the other, across 80 acres
handed down to me from my great grandfather, hog
farmer, Baptist, Populist. Sounds good, doesn't it? History
dreamy. From the front porch, looking down, at least the
field is accurate, except there was no wind and it was
wheat I rode through, astride a giant horse named Billy. I
was nine. I loved her, the smell of her sweat that lathered
up white around my legs in the heat. The slow way she
had of drinking water at the trough after work, sucking it
up through her great, yellow teeth that clicked sweetly the
whole time under those soft gray lips with the long hairs
on them. The trough lined in moss where beautiful blue
fish lived on the bottom. They were tiny in among the gold
motes. My nephew called them Jesus fish because it was
just luck if you saw one. My grandfather was bitter so he
didn't hand down anything. He was small in his bib overalls
and looked like one of those rotted out fence posts that
stands there only because the barbwire holds it up. He
took my penis out in a wheat field one day after we'd
eaten our lunch. You have to see me standing there near
Billy, the sun beating down, and his big hand pulling at
my pants. I concentrated on her, on the leather collar she
had to wear with the brass knobs I held on to, and the
black straps that followed the large curves of her body

down over the rump. Every evening he would hold up her
hooves, one at a time, while I dug out the hardpan packed
in around the frog. The thing is to remember Billy. And if
he's bad, don't say my grandfather doesn't matter or that
history stinks. You get the hay rake, don't you, and the
blackbirds coming in, ahead of schedule, over the field we
planted. What did you want? A new backhoe? God in the
poem? Some barred-rocks running around?

TOM CRAWFORD

The Bean Eaters

They eat beans mostly, this old yellow pair.
Dinner is a casual affair.
Plain chipware on a plain and creaking wood,
Tin flatware.

Two who are Mostly Good.
Two who have lived their day,
But keep on putting on their clothes
And putting things away.

And remembering . . .
Remembering, with twinklings and twinges,
As they lean over the beans in their rented back room that
    is full of beads and receipts and dolls and cloths,
    tobacco crumbs, vases and fringes.

GWENDOLYN BROOKS

Vespers

A linnet pulls a tuft of cowhair
snarled on barbed wire.
The threads of hair shine red-gold
in her beak. She flies into last light.

At the horizon earth & sky
reach a truce. The sun just down,
barn swallows tumble in the afterglow
above the slow turning windmill.
The hill darkens,

a saddle rubbed with oil,
not yet the complete black of Nevada night.
There's the soft whickering of a horse,
the flames of a hundred Asian poppies nodding red,
then the descending quiet.

GARY SHORT

III. Shanks, Sawgrass

Names of Horses

All winter your brute shoulders strained against collars, padding
and steerhide over the ash hames, to haul
sledges of cordwood for drying through spring and summer,
for the Glenwood stove next winter, and for the simmering range.

In April you pulled cartloads of manure to spread on the fields,
dark manure of Holsteins, and knobs of your own clustered with oats.
All summer you mowed the grass in meadow and hayfield, the mowing machine
clacketing beside you, while the sun walked high in the morning;

and after noon's heat, you pulled a clawed rake through the same acres,
gathering stacks, and dragged the wagon from stack to stack,
and the built hayrack back, uphill to the chaffy barn,
three loads of hay a day from standing grass in the morning.

Sundays you trotted the two miles to church with the light load
of a leather quartertop buggy, and grazed in the sounds of hymns.
Generation on generation, your neck rubbed the windowsill
of the stall, smoothing the wood as the sea smooths glass.

When you were old and lame, when your shoulders hurt
   bending to graze,
one October the man, who fed you and kept you, and
   harnessed you every morning,
led you through corn stubble to sandy ground above Eagle
   Pond,
and dug a hole beside you where you stood shuddering in
   your skin,

and lay the shotgun's muzzle in the boneless hollow
   behind your ear,
and fired the slug into your brain, and felled you into your
   grave,
shoveling sand to cover you, setting goldenrod upright
   above you,
where by next summer a dent in the ground made your
   monument.

For a hundred and fifty years, in the pasture of dead
   horses,
roots of pine trees pushed through the pale curves of your
   ribs,
yellow blossoms flourished above you in autumn, and in
   winter
frost heaved your bones in the ground—old toilers, soil
   makers:

O Roger, Mackerel, Riley, Ned, Nellie, Chester, Lady Ghost.

DONALD HALL

88

Near the Bravo 20 Bombing Range

I bring the mare a green apple, then ride
the wrinkled land along the river road
in the slow-turning wheel of the day.
Past the pen of the brown goat with the broken moan,
past the stiff glove thick with dirt
where it has lain on the path since winter,
past the coyote slung over the barbed fence,

its eyes gone to sky—
blue where a black jet angles
high above the stand of aspen, the leaves
spinning to coin in the wind's hand.
I ride past the green wave of alfalfa
that grows one sweet inch each day.

Over the next mountain is the range,
public land bombed for thirty-five unauthorized years.
At what point is turning back an option?
The skeleton of a mustang, dreaming its run,
rises slowly back out of dust.

Farther out, the surface of the marsh is sunstruck tin.
The ones who walked here before
walk quietly & believed the green
slick on the pond.
I hear the jet after it is gone.
What remains—a white strand, sheer against the sky,
with the breath of the mare
as she bends to drink
from the still water.

GARY SHORT

The Flying Change

1

The canter has two stride patterns, one on the right lead
and one on the left, each a mirror image of the other. The
leading foreleg is the last to touch the ground before the
moment of suspension in the air. On cantered curves, the
horse tends to lead with the inside leg. Turning at liberty,
he can change leads without effort during the moment of
suspension, but a rider's weight makes this more difficult.
The aim of teaching a horse to move beneath you is to
remind him how he moved when he was free.

2

A single leaf turns sideways in the wind
in time to save a remnant of the day;
I am lifted like a whipcrack to the moves
I studied on that barbered stretch of ground,
before I schooled myself to drift away

from skills I still possess, but must outlive.
Sometimes when I cup water in my hands
and watch it slip away and disappear,
I see that age will make my hands a sieve;
but for a moment the shifting world suspends

its flight and leans toward the sun once more,
as if to interrupt its mindless plunge
through works and days that will not come again.
I hold myself immobile in bright air,
sustained in time astride the flying change.

HENRY TAYLOR

Blackberry Light

Old man Wenzel, try to forget the yellow manure
    seeping from under your sick ewes,
        the mucus and cheesy matter
coughed up by tubercular cows,

exhaustion of plantings four times washed lost or blown
    lost,
        your Mrs. weeping softly
          all the way to sleep,

rats to drown from their tunnels under the hen roosts,
    blood-fat tics to singe from the dogs,
        wood to split and carry, garbage to bury
back of the fields behind the lordly maples,

bushels of dead chicks when your stove failed them,
    the ears of your rabbits infested with maggots,
        the eyes of your sheep struck blind by your sledge,

and the vapor of birth smells, the tastes
    of your own slaughtered lambs,
        the hayloft's only window where you sometimes sat
    alone,
light streaming in past cobwebs hooked with flies. . . .

Old man Wenzel, try to forget the parting loam,
    the spring morning's sun illumining
        your hunched-over, pale-green cotyledons,

and when, after rain, you leaned into dripping leaves,
    filled your palm with blackberries, and ate them,
        your whole farm vanishing for moments
of blackberry light behind your eyes,

the almost invisible, silvery tent-worms' rails
   along the apple limbs, those tiny lives,
      before you burned them, each evening returning

from branched world to central cocoon,
   their frail and perishable home.

WILLIAM HEYEN

Jim

The road winds over hills,
gullies between fields,
as we drive my mother's body
back to the town
where we were born,
and you tell me how most
of the family rode home
to lie for months
on the cot in the front room.
Pulling himself up for the
first time in weeks, Uncle Jim
washed, shaved, dressed in
white collar and tie—
and began his tale
at one in the morning—
your turn to listen.
And until the sun rose,
hunks of meat swayed back
and forth in his butcher shop.
Hooves dropped into stewpots,
intestines, scraped clean,
were stuffed again,
then found gleaming from
the faces of frying pans,
the odor rising through the house.
Jim claimed he knew all
there was about animals—
how hide clings to muscles,
how a heifer harbors
a fetus, how the udder
sags, abdomen bulges,

and the first sign she gives
is so human: a swelling
the shape of a hand.
Under the skin, you can
almost trace the bones
of the fingers, the lines
stretching back toward the ribs.
When the priest stretched
his palms over Jim,
you could not find a match
for the candles, you could
not shoo the old man's parakeets
back into their cage
or remember the prayers
as you knelt by the cot,
and you could not stop laughing,
the birds darting about,
your missal falling open,
Latin blurring, cotton settling
on Jim's eyes, nose, lips.
It was December,
the ground sealed by snow,
the wake put off until the thaw.
You waited all winter,
the body rolled in blankets
and stored in the hayloft,
then in March,
Uncle George brought
the corpse into the house,
stood it up in the corner
and poured whiskey down

its throat, then hands
shuffled through hands
and the squeeze-box wheezed
till early morning.
When the mourners finally
trickled out, once again
the storm door flew open,
clouds gathered, the wind
sang and you remembered
Jim ramble on about grass,
how it heals over old gullies,
how it deepens the color
of the soil, the shine of
the coat, the eye, and how
that eye keeps its shape
there on the butcher's block.
"You can see yourself upside
down in the lens," Jim said.
"Your own face stares back."

And the road winds back
to the Divide where
the prairie takes a breath
rising up into the sky.
Here are the fields where
Jim followed the harvest,
corn bending to oats
to wheat in the Dakotas.
Chaff and grain, steam
rushing out with the pop
and hiss of the thresher,

smokestack black,
the farm woman driving
the wagon, reins in hands,
doubling in pain, easing
herself down to the ground
where Jim reached in,
caught her son, wrapped him
in his shirt, dark with sweat.
Chaff and grain,
the day's stubble still
on his skin, that night
Jim stretched out in the
bunkhouse, pockets turned
inside out by bad bets,
and felt the sky darken
and close, press down,
heard the rain hammer the roof.
He wrote a letter home:
he claimed he knew all
there was about animals.

He drifted on west and found
an abandoned farmhouse in
Montana with everything
he wanted—curtains, rugs,
books, dishes in the cupboard.
He settled in, sowed a few
potatoes, split firewood
for the winter with the ax
left in the stump.
But whenever he rode into town,

children pointed and whispered,
"That's the one
who lives in the house."
At the barber's, he finally
heard the story.

Jim:
An old geezer lived all his life in that place.
Never spent a cent and had sacks of the stuff
stashed somewhere, maybe buried in the yard.
Well, one day a tramp wandered around looking
for work and the old man set him to chopping wood.
Soon, the tramp whistled the geezer over,
wanting him to see the bugs drilling holes in the logs.
"Soon, they'll chew through your whole house," the tramp
    said.
"What, where?" the geezer wrinkled up his face.
The tramp pointed. "There. Get down on your knees
and you'll see." The geezer got down on all fours,
wheeled his neck around, trying to see them bugs.
Then the tramp swung, bringing the ax down,
whacking off the old man's head. Next, the tramp
rummaged through everything—even dug holes
in the yard and didn't turn up a dime,
so he skedaddled out of town, never to be seen again.
But the geezer. They said the geezer stalked the house
at night and nobody dared step a foot in the place
until I stumbled along. But I didn't see nothing.
Not at first. Until one day when I was splitting wood,
up walks the geezer, holding his head in his hands.
Said he'd give me all his dough if I'd go after that tramp—

had one side of his nose all smashed in.
He took me inside and lifted up the hearthstone
and pulled out a little bag of coins. I galloped out
the next day never intending to do no looking for nobody,
but in Green River, Wyoming, I fell into a poker game
with this tall scrawny fellow who was snorting funny
from a twisted-up nose. He skunked me clean—
every last coin in the bag, then waltzed toward
the door with the loot. "Stop right there!" I yelled
and pulled my gun (not knowing what I was going
to do then), when in walks the geezer carrying his head.
The tramp takes one look at the blood dripping
on the floor, starts to shake and shimmy and drops
over backwards. Stone dead. Me, I gathered up the coins
and trotted on home to begin my butcher shop in this
    town.

And in the morning
he lay his head down and told
you how the body fattens,
opens, the blood drains,
the hide peels from the skull,
the pink tongue turning purple,
split in two like a piece
of pine, the one clean hole
in the forehead drawing
the darkness in. He told
how the fat is scraped off,
rolled into a ball and
hung from a tree in late
fall for the birds,

how the fields close,
the pheasants gleaning
the few last seeds,
how the earth turns under,
then an explosion of wings
flies up in front of your face.

MARY SWANDER

Short Story

My grandfather killed a mule with a hammer,
or maybe with a plank, or a stick, maybe
it was a horse—the story varied
in the telling. If he was planting corn
when it happened, it was a mule, and he was plowing
the upper slope, west of the house, his overalls
stiff to the knees with red dirt, the lines
draped behind his neck.
He must have been glad to rest
when the mule first stopped mid-furrow;
looked back at where he'd come, then down
to the brush along the creek he meant to clear.
No doubt he noticed the hawk's great leisure
over the field, the crows lumped
in the biggest elm on the opposite hill.
After he'd wiped his hatbrim with his sleeve,
he called to the mule as he slapped the line
along its rump, clicked and whistled.

My grandfather was a slight, quiet man,
smaller than most women, smaller
than his wife. Had she been in the yard,
seen him heading toward the pump now,
she'd pump for him a dipper of cold water.
Walking back to the field, past the corncrib,
he took an ear of corn to start the mule,
but the mule was planted. He never cursed
or shouted, only whipped it, the mule
rippling its backside each time
the switch fell, and when that didn't work
whipped it low on its side, where it's tender,

then cross-hatched the welts he'd made already.
The mule went down on one knee,
and that was when he reached for the blown limb,
or walked to the pile of seasoning lumber; or else,
unhooked the plow and took his own time to the shed
to get the hammer.
                        By the time I was born,
he couldn't even lift a stick. He lived
another fifteen years in a chair,
but now he's dead, and so is his son,
who never meant to speak a word against him,
and whom I never asked what his father
was planting and in which field,
and whether it happened before he married,
before his children came in quick succession,
before his wife died of the last one.
And only a few of us are left
who ever heard that story.

ELLEN BRYANT VOIGT

Barbed Wire

YOU JUST CUT THAT SOMBITCH
RIGHT HERE
—*Karl Kopp, Yarbrough Mountain*

It isn't no easy way
to find the endpiece of wore
onct it's in the roll
you can pick it up bounced it round
like this or roll it
upside the barn hard
mebbe it'll pop out
most times not
don't cost nothing to try
it was this man back home
name Johnny Ray Johnston
a inventer
he invented this thing it could help
find the endpiece
and sent it off to Warshington

he had this brother
name Haroldwayne Johnston
a blind gospel preacher
he wasn't always
he's a mean sonofabitch young
all filt up with sin and equity
fighting raising hell
had three four of them girls
his age up to the doctor
all before he's called
it was this other brother
name Leonas Timothy Johnston
he never learnt to read
so he got a job with the highway patrol
got shot by a shiner
I seen that worefinder

it worked my brother he bought one
where'd them pliers go?
so Haroldwayne one day
he's out in this field
where the neighbors run his hogs
hiding in the shinery
shooting a pellet gun
to watch them squolt and run
I guess hc was lessee
it was two years before he tried to heal
Mavis Tittle's one that died
of the toothache so he must of been twenty-four
goddam watch it
worell tear the hide right off
your hands you seen them gloves?

this storm come up a sudden
caught him out there
looking like a cyclone
he had to get home so he run
by the time he got to the fence
it was hailballs coming down
he tried to climb through with the gun
poached hisself
shot right up his nose
made all the blood go in his eyeballs
he's blind
that fence caught him
he's straddled of one wore
the top one had him grapt by the butt
here comes the storm
he sez he could feel that wore

go green when the lightening struct
made him a eunuch
he could look right at a naked womern
wouldn't nothing go down
nor come up after that
you find them pliers? look
in the jockey box or under the seat
sez he heard God call him

he'd been hollering like a sonofabitch
they heard all the way to the house
and was fixing to come but he quit
they waited till it quit raining
sez they'd of thought he's dead
and that would of made two
only one brother left for a seed crop
all that blood out his nose
except he's praying to hisself out loud
he never even heard them come up
it isn't none there? look
in the back see if it's some sidecutters
or something so they known he'd got religion
and they never seen he's even blind yet

he's a gospel preacher after
and Johnny Ray's a inventer
Leonas Timothy was arredy shot dead
what it was was a piece of wore
it could be fixed on the end at the store
except it was red paint on it
wherever the red was was the end
when you's through using wore

then fix the red one on
next time there'd be the endpiece red
Haroldwayne he saved hundreds of lostsouls
come all over to hear him heal
best on headaches and biliousness
it was one family had this crippled boy
come about eighty miles to see him gospel preach
brung this boy up front
he taken and grapt his head
hollers the words and sez now walk
but he fell on his ast still crippled
they sez it wasn't Haroldwayne's fault
them people didn't have faith
I heard he drownt a year or two after that

the govament never did send Johnny Ray
no patent agreement we figgered
he kept the invention for hisself
so Johnny Ray he made some up
and sold to his friends around town
you caint buy it nowhere else
I wisht I had one now
I've waste more damn time on wore today
than I have to lose
bring them pliers here
let's cut this sonofabitch it don't matter where
we gone set here all day
won't never get this damn fence done

DAVID LEE

Blue Corn, Black Mesa

Before you go, I need to tell you
why here tongues turn dry as piki bread.
No one knows why this story is true

but I know there was a woman who
buried both hands in blue dough. She said,
Before you go, I need to tell you

why Hopi corn grows short, in a few
spindly clumps, not deep and wide and red.
No one knows why this story is true,

but I know it is not a lie. New
seed lay still; the sheep we gave for dead.
Before you go I need to tell you

that crater's spirit gave us breath. Blue
winds swept ash from the mesa, it bled—
no one knows why this story is true—

earth's sky blood washed ragged furrows. Blue
corn cracked, tucked sharp in this lava bed.
Before you go, I need to tell you:
no one knows why this story is true.

PEGGY SHUMAKER

The First Birth

I had not been there before where the vagina opens,
the petals of liver, each vein a delicate bush,
and where something clutches its way into the light
like a mummy tearing and fumbling from his shroud.
The heifer was too small, too young in the hips,
short-bodied with outriggers distending her sides,
and back in the house, in the blue *Giants of Science*
still open on my bed, Ptolemy was hurtling toward
    Einstein.
Marconi was inventing the wireless without me.
Da Vinci was secretly etching the forbidden anatomy
of the Dark Ages. I was trying to remember
Galen, his pen drawing, his inscrutable genius,
not the milk in the refrigerator, sour with bitterweed.
It came, cream-capped and hay-flecked, in silver pails.
At nights we licked onions to sweeten the taste.
All my life I had been around cows named after friends
and fated for slaughterhouses. I wanted to bring
Mendel and Rutherford into that pasture,
and bulb-headed Hippocrates, who would know what
    to do.
The green branch nearby reeked of crawfish.
The heavy horseflies orbited. A compass, telescope,
and protractor darted behind my eyes. When the sac
broke, the water soaked one thigh. The heifer lowed.
Enrico Fermi, how much time it takes, the spotted legs,
the wet black head and white blaze. The shoulders
lodged. The heifer walked with the calf wedged
in her pelvis, the head swaying behind her like a cut
    blossom.

Did I ever go back to science, or eat a hamburger
without that paralysis, that hour of the stuck calf
and the unconscionable bawling that must have been a
    prayer?
Now that I know a little it helps, except for birth
or dying, those slow pains, like the rigorous observation
of Darwin. Anyway, I had to take the thing, any way
I could, as my hands kept slipping, wherever it was,
under the chin, by tendony, china-delicate knees,
my foot against the hindquarters of the muley heifer,
to bring into this world, black and enormous,
wobbling to his feet, the dumb bull, Copernicus.

RODNEY JONES

During the First Three Minutes of Life

The piglet
sucks

naps
wakes up

sniffs
the nipple next door

bites
his brother's ear

naps again
snores

wakes up
shivers

jumps straight up
twists an ankle

squeals
looks around for the sound

leaves home
gets lost`

pees
on the run

stops on a window
frame of light

looks up
into the sun

JIM HEYNEN

The Sow Piglet's Escapes

When the little sow piglet squirmed free,
Gus and I ran her all the way down to the swamp
and lunged and floundered and fell full-length
on our bellies stretching for her—and got her!—
and lay there, all three shining with swamp slime—
she yelping, I laughing, Gus—it was then I knew
he would die soon—gasping and gasping.
She made her second escape on the one day
when she was just big enough to dig an escape hole
and still small enough to squeeze through it.
Every day for the next week I took a bucket of meal
to her plot of rooted-up ground in the woods,
until one day there she was, waiting for me,
the wild beast evidently all mealed out of her.
She trotted over and let me stroke her back
and, dribbling corn down her chin, put up her little
    worried face
as if to remind me not to forget to recapture her—
though, really, a pig's special alertness to death
ought to have told her: in Sheffield the *dolce vita*
leads to the Lyndonville butcher. But when I seized her
she wriggled hard and cried, *wee wee wee,* all the way
    home.

GALWAY KINNELL

Cutting the Easter Colt

This saddlebag surgeon readies his tools
like a Monsignor prepares
for communion. Holy day or not,
nothing's sacrilegious
when the moon comes
ripe, the disinfectant fumes
stunning us hard as incense
at high mass. We lead
the stud, procession-like, into the corral,
scotch-hobble and throw him
fast with cotton ropes, then watch
this wrangler/pastor/sawbones—all-
arounder—move his 55 years of heart
and savvy, lickety-split
amid thrashing hooves
to lash all 4 together
at the pasterns. He swashes
the scrotum, a glistening lobed
world, delicate and thin-veined—perfect
contrast to his saddlemaker hands,
fingers braided like rawhide bosals,
his knuckles the thick heel knots.
With knife honed to a featheredge,
he makes the incision and probes
until he hunts both down,
an Easter egg apiece for the blue
heeler pups, their anxious panting
reflected in the gold
chalice of the gelding's eye.

PAUL ZARZYSKI

The Vealers

They come forth with all four legs folded in
like a dime-store card table.
Their hides are watered silk.
As in blindman's buff they rise, unable
to know except by touch, and begin
to root from side to side in search of milk.

The stanchions hang empty. Straw beds the planks
that day. On that day they are left at will
to nuzzle and malinger
under the umbrella of their mothers' flanks
sucking from those four fingers
they were called forth to fill.

Immediately thereafter each is penned
narrowly and well, like a Strasbourg goose.
Milk comes on schedule in a nippled pail.
It is never enough to set them loose
from that birthday dividend
of touch. Bleating racks the jail.

Across the barn the freshened cows
answer until they forget who is there.
Morning and night, machinery
empties their udders. Grazing allows
them to refill. The hungry
calves bawl and doze sucking air.

The sponges of their muzzles pucker
and grow wet with nursing dreams.
In ten weeks' time the knacker

—the local slaughterer—will back his truck
against the ramp, and prodded to extremes
they will kick and buck

and enter
and in our time they will come forth for good
dead center
wrapped and labeled in a plastic sheet,
their perfect flesh unstreaked with blood
or muscle, and we will eat.

MAXINE KUMIN

Strut

Every morning to guard against glut I chop
zucchini zealots for the lambs
who are not particularly grateful.
They prefer old apples and fresh grain.

Every morning I rethink how common green
—pond scum, a thousand sumac sprouts
brome and rye grass, birdsfoot trefoil
milkweed, poke, dock, dill, sorrell

bush and shrub, soft and hardwoods, all
leafy headed—must go down again in
frost and come again. Is this a deep
head-tilting meditative thought, or

vernal instinctual, nothing more?
Here come the marbleized rat-wet new foals
blowing blue bubbles like divers into air
on their feet in minutes finding

the mares' teats by trial-and-error blind
butting stagger-dance. And here comes
cakewalk cocky with the whole mess
of birth and rebirth the strut of the season.

Almost bliss.

MAXINE KUMIN

115

Hay for the Horses

He had driven half the night
From far down San Joaquin
Through Mariposa, up the
Dangerous mountain roads,
And pulled in at eight a.m.
With his big truckload of hay
    behind the barn.
With winch and ropes and hooks
We stacked the bales up clean
To splintery redwood rafters
High in the dark, flecks of alfalfa
Whirling through shingle-cracks of light,
Itch of haydust in the
    sweaty shirt and shoes.
At lunchtime under Black oak
Out in the hot corral,
—The old mare nosing lunchpails,
Grasshoppers crackling in the weeds—
"I'm sixty-eight" he said,
"I first bucked hay when I was seventeen.
I thought, that day I started,
I sure would hate to do this all my life.
And dammit, that's just what
I've gone and done."

GARY SNYDER

116

The Horse

He'd rent the horse and it sounding like it had asthma
and its legs shivery
and its back dropped so far your feet dragged
on the ground when you sat on it
even if you was the youngest,

he'd rent it,
touching it on its side all the way down to its tail
and back up to its neck,
picking its feet up, squinting into its face,
prying open its mouth: horse,

it was after all
a horse
and all he needed was what it was
harnessed to the plough for a couple of afternoons,
he had a hand cultivator but it was hard,
slow work; that horse,

I always waited for it to die the way it shook
and wheezed,
and he'd hit it with the harness straps
and swear at it and say he could surely do it faster,
and it would pull and rattle at the harness
and he'd have his sleeves rolled up
and be hauling back on the plough,
pulling against the horse, and the ploughshares
would dig
into the dirt
and get stuck, and he'd have the harness wrapped
around him and in his hands as well as the plough

handles, his feet braced and his legs stiff,
his hat pulled deep on his forehead,
cussing his luck for having thought to do it
this way when he had good strong kids
could pull better, the horse too old

and sick to care, and him sweatier, and finally
so mad he wasn't mad at all,
his lips tight and disappeared right off
his face and his arms lumpy with his veins
all knotted out in his skin
and his shoes unlaced and full of dirt,

him more buried and turned over than the earth,
stiff-legged and measuring nothing with his eyes
like he had done when he began,
not looking
at where the sun stood in the sky and how long

it would take to do this much and then
that much and by mid-afternoon,
if he was lucky, maybe this part here
and that would leave over there and back behind that
little U in the trees to do.
Nothing. His eyes
straight ahead and on the horse's backside,
blinking the sweat loose sometimes
but mostly letting it settle and roll down
his eyes, not looking anywhere,
turning the horse around,
pulling on the plough, loosening it,

holding onto the animal and turning it all
around
to walk back up again, dipping the ploughshares
and pushing them
so that they were into the ground
and could claw it up
and out and him

as tired by the time she made him quit
as the horse had been when he had started,
giving him water and looking at him suspicious
and cautious of his mood
and what she could do to make it better
so he wouldn't be mad supper was late
when we got home, and him saying

if that horse died
on his land, the man who owned it
had better come and clear it off
and pay him back his money
and money besides for the time lost
looking at his goddamn dead horse,
whatever possessed him to think he needed
to use it, anyway.

He'd say it as he untied the harness straps
from around his back and arms and hands,
looking down at it like he hadn't never seen it
before and didn't know maybe
it belonged on trees
or should be thrown in the water

or used in the house somehow in the winter
near the stove, it so heavy and useless,
he spoke

so flat and low with no heat in his voice,
it all burned out of him by the sun
and the work he'd done and have to do again
tomorrow and probably, by the looks of it,
the next day, too,

and he'd heard there were better ways to live,
better ways, with only looking at the fields
from automobile windows as you drove
along beside them
and pointed out the window
and wondered what that hillbilly was doing,
and he was tired
and tired
of being tied to this useless hide
of dog food all the days of his life,
and to this small patch of land—
worthless was what it was—
and he'd drink

from the dipper and us crowded together
back where he couldn't reach us with the harness straps
if he should try, looking
at him and at her, knowing she'd handle it,
she'd even out his temper before we took the horse
back and headed for home ourselves.

And as we went back
and it darkening
his mood toward the horse
changed
and he wasn't so sour toward it, it did the best
it could, old and lame
and sick as it was. The air

was cooler
and his body and legs weren't so knotted up
nor his arms,
his sleeves rolled down, his hat
pushed back on his head, the day
didn't hurt so much thinking about it
as we walked in the slow dark
toward home.

FAYE KICKNOSWAY

Somewhere along the Way

You lean on a wire fence, looking across
a field of grain with a man you have stopped
to ask for directions. You are not lost.
You stopped here only so you could take a moment
to see whatever this old farmer sees
who crumbles heads of wheat between his palms.

Rust is lifting the red paint from his barn roof,
and earth hardens over the sunken arc
of his mower's iron wheel. All his sons
have grown and moved away, and the old woman
keeps herself in the parlor where the light
is always too weak to make shadows. He sniffs

at the grain in his hand, and cocks an ear
toward a dry tree ringing with cicadas.
There are people dying today, he says,
that never died before. He lifts an arm
and points, saying what you already knew
about the way you are trying to go;

you nod and thank him, and think of going on,
but only after you have stood and listened
a little while longer to the soft click
of the swaying grain heads soon to be cut,
and the low voice, edged with dim prophecy,
that settles down around you like the dust.

HENRY TAYLOR

The Bull God

The bull god moves from sunlight
Into shade, following the drool of his snout
To what he needs. Day after day the rhythm
Of his blood consumes him, his enormous
Body a gentle blue desire.

He stands for hours
In the August sun, flies weaving
A dark crown above his massive head
As he waits for the next flutter of delight
To stir the heavy neurons of his brain
And start again the oblivious lumbering
From pleasure to pleasure. The long
Slow nerve of his body touched
By the scent of bulrushes and black mud.

And rubbing against the half rotted
Post of a fence the coarse hide of his
Ponderous belly, he walks slowly away
Into the insect-singing heat, his great balls
Swaying behind him like heavy stones,
His ancient, swaggering cock as tense
With seed as a milkweed pod about to burst
With the next touch of the wind.

JOE SALERNO

Uncle George

Some catastrophes are better than others.
Wheat under the snow lived by blizzards
that massacred stock on Uncle George's farm.
Only telephone poles remember the place, and the wire
thrills a mile at a time into that intent blast
where the wind going by fascinated whole
millions of flakes and thousands of acres of tumbleweeds.

There in the spring birds will come measuring along
their nesting stream where I like to go hunt through the
    snow
for furred things that wait and survive. Trapper
of warm sight, I plow and belong, send breath
to be part of the day, and where it arrives
I spend on and on, fainter and fainter
toward ultimate identification, joining the air
a few breaths at a time. I test a bough
that held, last year, but this year may come down.

The cold of Uncle George's farm I carry home in my
overcoat, where I live reluctantly one life at a time;
like one driven on, I flutter, measure my stream
by many little calls: "Oh, Uncle George—where you
poured the chicken feed!—where you broke open
the window screen for the nesting swallow!—where the
    barn
held summer and winter against that slow blizzard, the
    sky!"

WILLIAM STAFFORD

124

For the Eating of Swine

I have learned sloppiness from an old sow
wallowing her ennui in the stinking lot,
a slow vessel filled with a thousand candles,
her whiskers matted with creek mud,
her body helpless to sweat the dull spirit.
I have wrestled the hindquarters of a young boar
while my father clipped each testicle
with a sharpened Barlow knife, returning him,
good fish, to his watery, changed life.
And I have learned pleasure from a gilt
as she lay on her back, offering her soft belly
like a dog, the loose bowel of her throat
opening to warble the consonants of her joy.
I have learned lassitude, pride, stubbornness,
and greed from my many neighbors, the pigs.
I have gone with low head and slanted blue eyes
through the filthy streets, wary of the blade,
my whole life, a toilet or kitchen,
the rotting rinds, the wreaths of flies.
For the chicken, the cow, forgetfulness. Mindlessness
blesses their meat. Only the pigs are holy,
the rings in their snouts, their fierce, motherly indignation,
and their need always to fill themselves.
I remember a photograph. A sheriff had demolished
a still, spilling a hundred gallons of moonshine.
Nine pigs passed out in the shade of a mulberry tree.
We know pigs will accommodate
demons, run into rivers, drowning of madness.
They will devour drunks who fall in their ways.
Like Christ, they will befriend their destroyers.
In the middle of winter I have cupped my hands

and held the large and pliable brain of a pig.
As the fires were heating the black kettles,
I have scrupulously placed my rifle between pigs' eyes
and with one clean shot loosened the slabs
of side-meat, the sausages that begin
with the last spasms of the trotters.
O dolphins of the barnyard, frolickers
in the gray and eternal muck, in all your parts
useful, because I have known you, this is the sage,
and salt, the sacrificial markers of pepper.
What pity should I feel, or gratitude, raising you
on my fork as all the dead shall be risen?

RODNEY JONES

Saint Francis and the Sow

The bud
stands for all things,
even for those things that don't flower,
for everything flowers, from within, of self-blessing;
though sometimes it is necessary
to reteach a thing its loveliness,
to put a hand on its brow
of the flower
and retell it in words and in touch
it is lovely
until it flowers again from within, of self-blessing;
as Saint Francis
put his hand on the creased forehead
of the sow, and told her in words and in touch
blessings of earth on the sow, and the sow
began remembering all down her thick length,
from the earthen snout all the way
through the fodder and slops to the spiritual curl of the
    tail,
from the hard spininess spiked out from the spine
down through the great broken heart
to the blue milken dreaminess spurting and shuddering
from the fourteen teats into the fourteen mouths sucking
    and blowing beneath them:
the long, perfect loveliness of sow.

GALWAY KINNELL

Earth Dweller

It was all the clods at once become
precious; it was the barn, and the shed,
and the windmill, my hands, the crack
Arlie made in the axe handle: oh, let me stay
here humbly, forgotten, to rejoice in it all;
let the sun casually rise and set.
If I have not found the right place,
teach me; for, somewhere inside, the clods are
vaulted mansions, lines through the barn sing
for the saints forever, the shed and windmill
rear so glorious the sun shudders like a gong.

Now I know why people worship, carry around
magic emblems, wake up talking dreams
they teach to their children: the world speaks.
The world speaks everything to us.
It is our only friend.

WILLIAM STAFFORD

Farmer

Seasons waiting the miracle,
dawn after dawn framing
the landscape in his eyes:

bound tight as wheat, packed
hard as dirt. Made shrewd
by soil and weather, through

the channel of his bones
shift ways of animals,
their matings twist his dreams.

While night-fields quicken,
shadows slanting right, then left
across the moonlit furrows,

he shelters in the farmhouse
merged with trees, a skin of wood,
as much the earth's as his.

LUCIEN STRYK

Barn Fire

It starts, somehow, in the hot damp
and soon the lit bales
throb in the hayloft. The tails

of mice quake in the dust,
the bins of grain, the mangers stuffed
with clover, the barrels of oats
shivering individually in their pale

husks—animate and inanimate: they know
with the first whiff in the dark.
And we knew, or should have: that day
the calendar refused its nail

on the wall and the crab apples hurling
themselves to the ground ... Only moments
and the flames like a blue fist curl

all around the black. There is some
small blaring from the calves and the cows'
nostrils flare only once
more, or twice, above the dead dry

metal troughs. ... No more fat tongues worrying
the salt licks, no more heady smells
of deep green from silos rising now

like huge twin chimneys above all this.
With the lofts full there is no stopping
nor even getting close: it will rage

until dawn and beyond,—and the horses,
because they know they are safe there,
the horses run back into the barn.

THOMAS LUX

IV. Open Furrows

Hard Red Wheat

"When it makes the shovel ring,"
his dad sang, "it's ripe!"
In Glasgow, Montana, he raises grain
on land where his father taught him:
plow, harrow, seed, and wait
for the disappearing act
of green, at its leisure, in siesta
August heat—that friction
and sizzle, times a jillion,
of a single head he threshes
between cricket-motion
anxious hands, then winnows
in a whiff of breath. Seed almost dry,
he brooms out the bins, the big
dipper spouted over them
in a stainless sky. He dreams
bushels of augered stars,
green and yellow revolutions
of his John Deere combine
luring him into sleep
so hypnotic
only hail against the panes
snaps him from it. He looks north
for nightmare corduroy—purple
cloud—south, where grain ripens first,
for neighbors, harvesting
horizon strips. He cuts
a swath, cups a sifting handful
from the hopper, pinches one kernel
between eyeteeth, and smiles

at his spaniel's fandango
in the wheat, leap after salmon
leap through rapids—pirouettes
engraved in red gold he knows
today will make that shovel ring.

For Al Knaff

PAUL ZARZYSKI

Emergency Haying

Coming home with the last load I ride standing
on the wagon tongue, behind the tractor
in hot exhaust, lank with sweat,

my arms strung
awkwardly along the hayrack, cruciform.
Almost 500 bales we've put up

this afternoon, Marshall and I.
And of course I think of another who hung
like this on another cross. My hands are torn

by baling twine, not nails, and my side is pierced
by my ulcer, not a lance. The acid in my throat
is only hayseed. Yet exhaustion and the way

my body hangs from twisted shoulders, suspended
on two points of pain in the rising
monoxide, recall that greater suffering.

Well, I change grip and the image
fades. It's been an unlucky summer. Heavy rains
brought on the grass tremendously, a monster crop,

but wet, always wet. Haying was long delayed.
Now is our last chance to bring in
the winter's feed, and Marshall needs help.

We mow, rake, bale, and draw the bales
to the barn, these late, half-green,
improperly cured bales; some weigh 100 pounds

or more, yet must be lugged by the twine
across the field, tossed on the load, and then
at the barn unloaded on the conveyor

and distributed in the loft. I help—
I, the desk-servant, work-worker—
and hold up my end pretty well too; but God,

the close of day, how I fall down then. My hands
are sore, they flinch when I light my pipe.
I think of those who have done slave labor,

less able and less well prepared than I.
Rose Marie in the rye fields of Saxony,
her father in the camps of Moldavia

and the Crimea, all clerks and housekeepers
herded to the gaunt fields of torture. Hands
too bloodied cannot bear

even the touch of air, even
the touch of love. I have a friend
whose grandmother cut cane with a machete

and cut and cut, until one day
she snicked her hand off and took it
and threw it grandly at the sky. Now

in September our New England mountains
under a clear sky for which we're thankful at last
begin to glow, maples, beeches, birches

in their first color. I look
beyond our famous hayfields to our famous hills,
to the notch where the sunset is beginning,

then in the other direction, eastward,
where a full new-risen moon like a pale
medallion hangs in a lavender cloud

beyond the barn. My eyes
sting with sweat and loveliness. And who
is the Christ now, who

if not I? It must be so. My strength
is legion. And I stand up high
on the wagon tongue in my whole bones to say

woe to you, watch out
you sons of bitches who would drive men and women
to the fields where they can only die.

HAYDEN CARRUTH

The Elements of San Joaquin

Field

The wind sprays pale dirt into my mouth
The small, almost invisible scars
On my hands.

The pores in my throat and elbows
Have taken in a seed of dirt of their own.

After a day in the grape fields near Rolinda
A fine silt, washed by sweat,
Has settled into the lines
On my wrists and palms.

Already I am becoming the valley,
A soil that sprouts nothing
For any of us.

Wind

A dry wind over the valley
Peeled mountains, grain by grain,
To small slopes, loose dirt
Where red ants tunnel.

The wind strokes
The skulls and spines of cattle
To white dust, to nothing,

Covers the spiked tracks of beetles,
Of tumbleweed, of sparrows
That pecked the ground for insects.

Evenings, when I am in the yard weeding,
The wind picks up the breath of my armpits
Like dust, swirls it
Miles away

And drops it
On the ear of a rabid dog,
And I take on another life.

Sun

In June the sun is a bonnet of light
Coming up,
Little by little,
From behind a skyline of pine.

The pastures sway with fiddle-neck
Tassels of foxtail.

At Piedra
A couple fish on the river's edge,
Their shadows deep against the water.
Above, in the stubbled slopes,
Cows climb down
As the heat rises
In a mist of blond locusts,
Returning to the valley.

GARY SOTO

Hoeing

During March while hoeing long rows
Of cotton
Dirt lifted in the air
Entering my nostrils
And eyes
The yellow under my fingernails

The hoe swung
Across my shadow   chopping weeds
And thick caterpillars
That shriveled
Into rings
And went where the wind went

When the sun was on the left
And against my face
Sweat   the sea
That is still within me
Rose and fell from my chin
Touching land
For the first time

GARY SOTO

142

Field Poem

When the foreman whistled
My brother and I
Shouldered our hoes,
Leaving the field.
We returned to the bus
Speaking
In broken English, in broken Spanish
The restaurant food,
The tickets to a dance
We wouldn't buy with our pay.

From the smashed bus window,
I saw the leaves of cotton plants
Like small hands
Waving good-bye.

GARY SOTO

Plowing

1

All my life. Broken ground.
Shovels. John Deere bangers. Sticks, cats, hoes
always forgotten people speak
old ways, lost ways, fossils.

I found an old plow
bought leather straps, borrowed John's
half blind Dan *n goddamit boy*
don let that sonnybitch kick ya he's mean bastard
sed John, helped me with harness.

2

My anticipations all misplaced,
early plowed under. Expected sun
and flesh, tracings and neck leaders
mind drifting to Kolob's breezes,
tired arms, hoarse throat.

Found wind, thick clods. John's Dan
walked easy, followed his good eye
in straight lines. I moved, something habitual,
behind, stepping over turned earth
shy at harness
precariously balanced on one of the world's edges
wind against my hair
exploding into afternoon *god aint he sumin*
that mule's so old he carried Moses inta Jewsalem

and he aint forgot a goddam thang
wind and earth and animal
the only geometry.

3

All my life I've heard death
takes us to the cycle's center,
where we should be, crystals
clusters. We exist within, know
both sides at once. Perfect definition.

And that life is broken parabola.
We wander against wind, random circles,
no closer to center, glimpses,
shadows and edges *I caint tell ya how to do it boy*
its gonna be there in ya bones or it aint shit for
     nowhere
the world inside. And I followed John's mule
my boots relaxed in stillness, shattered dust

plowed earth, wind, sky.
And John walked beside, talked of hog markets
hollow bones, lakebottoms and forgotten ways.
The moon swallowed dusk. Our image
crystalized against a backdrop of night.

DAVID LEE

The Drought

The clouds shouldered a path up the mountains
East of Ocampo, and then descended,
Scraping their bellies gray on the cracked shingles of slate.

They entered the valley, and passed the roads that went
Trackless, the houses blown open, their cellars creaking
And lined with the bottles that held their breath for years.

They passed the fields where the trees dried thin as hat
   racks
And the plow's tooth bit the earth for what endured.
But what continued were the wind that plucked the birds
   spineless

And the young who left with a few seeds in each pocket,
Their belts tightened on the fifth notch of hunger—
Under the sky that deafened from listening for rain.

GARY SOTO

Mud

You would think that the little birches
would die of that brown mouth sucking
and sucking their root ends.
The rain runs yellow.
The mother pumps in, pumps in
more than she can swallow.
All of her pockmarks spill over.
The least footfall
brings up rich swill.

The streams grow sick with their tidbits.
The trout turn up their long bellies.
The slugs come alive. An army
of lips works in its own ocean.
The boulders gape to deliver themselves.
Stones will be born of that effort.

Meanwhile the mother is sucking.
Pods will startle apart,
pellets be seized with a fever
and as the dark gruel thickens,
life will stick up a finger.

MAXINE KUMIN

Roots

call it our craziness even,
call it anything.
it is the life thing in us
that will not let us die.
even in death's hand
we fold the fingers up
and call them greens and
grow on them,
we hum them and make music.
call it our wildness then,
we are lost from the field
of flowers, we become
a field of flowers.
call it our craziness
our wildness
call it our roots,
it is the light in us
it is the light of us
it is the light, call it
whatever you have to,
call it anything.

LUCILLE CLIFTON

To Ms. Ann

i will have to forget
your face
when you watched me breaking
in the fields,
missing my children.

i will have to forget
your face
when you watched me carry
your husband's
stagnant water.

i will have to forget
your face
when you handed me
your house
to make a home,

and you never called me sister
then, you never called me sister
and it has only been forever and
i will have to forget your face.

LUCILLE CLIFTON

I Once Knew a Man

i once knew a man who had wild horses killed.
when he told about it
the words came galloping out of his mouth
and shook themselves and headed off in
every damn direction. his tongue
was wild and wide and spinning when he talked
and the people he looked at closed their eyes
and tore the skins off their backs as they walked away
and stopped eating meat.
there was no holding him once he got started;
he had had wild horses killed one time and
they rode him to his grave.

LUCILLE CLIFTON

Cornpicker Poem

I

Sheds left out in the darkness,
Abandoned granaries, cats merging into the night.

There are hubcaps cooling in the dark yard.

The stiff-haired son has slouched in
And gone to bed.
A low wind sweeps over the moony land.

II

Overshoes stiffen in the entry.
The calendar grows rigid on the wall.

He dreams, and his body grows limber.
He is fighting a many-armed woman;
He is a struggler, he will not yield.
He fights her in the crotch of a willow tree.

He wakes up with jaws set,
And a victory.

III

It is dawn. Cornpicking today.
He leans over, hurtling
His old Pontiac down the road.

Somewhere the sullen chilled machine
Is waiting, its empty gas cans around it.

ROBERT BLY

Harvest

East of the sun's slant, in the vineyard that never failed,
A wind crossed my face, moving the dust
And a portion of my voice a step closer to a new year.

The sky went black in the 9th hour of rolling trays,
And in the distance ropes of rain dropped to pull me
From the thick harvest that was not mine.

GARY SOTO

The Orchard Keeper

Snow has fallen on snow for two days behind the Keilen farmhouse.... When we put our ears down, near the snow, we hear the sound the porgies hear near the ocean floor, the note the racer hears the moment before his death, the chord that lifts the buoyant swimmer in the channel.

Four pigeon-grass bodies, scarce and fine, sway above the snow. The heron walks dawdling on long legs in white morning fog; a musical thought rises as the pianist sits down at her table; the body labors before dawn to understand its dream.

In its dream, thin legs come down the mountainside, hooves clatter over the wooden bridge, go along a wall, eyes look in at the orchard. Near the well at the center, four men lie stretched out sleeping; each man's sword lies under him. And the orchard keeper, where is he?

ROBERT BLY

The Cherry

February: the season grips—
 heavy—the chomped
stalks in Miller's field
 across the way.

Wind comes level, spurred by
 western counties,
and horses our daughter watched
 all summer long

shiver in woodland now. Below,
 piled branches
downed by the storm of mid-December
 shift in the gusts.

We have waited a month for the city
 to cart them off—
it's been so cold the ice that
 let the storm strip

clean, has scarcely thawed. The day
 those branches split
I had to axe the cherry to its roots.
 Our girl, sulking

out of range, held tight to twigs.

LUCIEN STRYK

In the Farmhouse

1

Eaves moan,
clapboards flap,

behind me the potbellied
stove
Ironside #120, rusty, cracked,
rips thick chunks of birchwood
into fire.

2

Soon it will be spring,
again the vanishing of the snows,

and tonight
I sit up late, mouthing
the sounds that would be words
in this flimsy jew's-harp of a farmhouse
in the wind
rattling on the twelve lights of blackness.

GALWAY KINNELL

Mood Indigo

From the porch; from the hayrick where her prickled
brothers hid and chortled and slurped into their young
   pink
lungs the ash-blond dusty air that lay above the bales

like low clouds; and from the squeak and suck
of the well pump, and from the glove of rust it implied
on her hand; from the dress parade of clothes

in her mothproofed closet; from her tiny Philco
with its cracked speaker and Sunday litany
("Nick Carter," "The Shadow," "Sky King");

from the loosening bud of her body; from hunger,
as they say; and from reading; from the finger
she used to dial her own number; from the dark

loam of the harrowed fields and from the very sky—
it came from everywhere. Which is to say it was
always there, and that it came from nowhere.

It evaporated with the dew, and at dusk when dark
spread in the sky like water in a blotter it spread, too,
but it came back and curdled with milk and stung

with nettles. It was in the bleat of a lamb, the way
a clapper is in a bell, and in the raucous, scratchy
gossip of the crows. It walked with her to school and lay

with her to sleep and at last she was well pleased.
If she were to sew, she would prick her finger with it.
If she were to bake, it would linger in the kitchen

like an odor snarled in the deepest folds of childhood.
It became her dead pet, her lost love, the baby sister
blue and dead at birth, the chill headwaters of the river

that purled and meandered and ran and ran until
it issued into her, as into a sea, and then she was its
and it was wholly hers. She kept to her room, as we

learned to say, but now and then she'd come down
and pass through the kitchen, and the screen door
would close behind her with no more sound than

an envelope being sealed, and she'd walk for hours
in the fields like a lithe blue rain, and end up
in the barn, and one of us would go and bring her in.

WILLIAM MATTHEWS

158

The Lonely One

The lonely one I be.
I sit on top of the highest hill above the valley.
Looking down towards my hogan, and the pastures.
Wondering how beautiful it used to be.
Green pastures with cattle and horses in it.
Now, it's all gone.
It's like the light of my life is gone.
No bird to listen to, only the forgotten
conversation, comes back to me.
I sit here as the wind caresses my sadden face.
I am waiting for a new beginning each day.
I am the lonely one.

RONALD JUMBO

The Farm

We sold it. To a man
who would be a patriarch.
I told John we were closed in,
subdivisions and trailers all around,
complaints of the smell (though
there was none), Ira came out
and told me to keep them fenced
(though none broke out), the neighbors
frightened because someone's cousin's
friend heard of a hog
that ate a child who fell in the pen (though
their children rode my sows
at feeding time), because I was tired,
because Jan carried our child and could
no longer help, because she wanted a home.

And the patriarch lost his first crop
to weeds, threw a rod in the tractor,
dug a basement and moved the trailer on
for extra bedrooms, cut the water lines
for a ditch, subdivided the farm
and sold the pigs for sausage. I told John
they were his, they were no longer mine,
I couldn't be responsible.

The wire connecting our voices was silent
for a moment. "You stupid sonofabitch," was all
he finally said. "You poor stupid bastard."

DAVID LEE

Earth Closet

Not much bigger than a dollhouse raised
in the hemlock shade,
the out-closet greens with moss.
The door opens on a chest with holes
and closes on a booth of calling space.
The spiders in corners are affluent with flies.
Needles seep through the cracks and have to be
swept from the seats.
Look down into the lime-frozen pit.
Except for the creak of the spruce pine
polishing the roof, you're alone
with the pause of earth—hillflesh
raw beneath. The enhoused shrine
spreads batter downhill crusting at the edges,
becoming dirt. Smell of the dank catalogue.
The excess is thrown as in a wishing pool
and, the daily toll of soil rendered
to soil in the rites of earth,
the watchman's box is left
its closeness inside the weather.

ROBERT MORGAN

161

These Obituaries of Rattlesnakes
Being Eaten by the Hogs

1

The arthritic farmer and a calf watch Dr. Graves
punch a needle into the jugular
of a cow with milkfever, and feed
calcium salts from a jar into a surgical tube. I wonder
at the flat maroon afterbirth of the night before, the
      farmer's
tobacco pouch, and the brown saliva of 6 a.m. on his lip.

In a booth at The Grill I order wheat
cakes and tea, the vet
a waffle and a tuna-fish sandwich. He shouldn't
tell me this but every time he looks up at the cookie-
punched tin ceiling he sees the farmer, his child stumbling
into the bailer, how he found her leg sticking out of the
      hay,
went home for his scattergun, and blew his brains into a
      burlap bag.

Standing in a manure gutter holding a heifer by the ears
over the wood slats of a manger, a farmer's wife, with
sour cream on her breath, asks what's my name, my
      business
in life, tells me that all this must be very
inspiring, and when the heifer's nose, clamped and tied to
      a beam, starts
to pull away from her face, I pass the tattooer, the syringe,
and the ink to the vet and say it is, Mrs. Hochstetler, it is.
"Then why don't you get out of the light so he can write
      the bill."

About two instruments with funny names: the twitch and
    White's
improved emasculator. The twitch is a bat with a loop tied
    at one end

while you run a lubricated tube down a nostril into the
    belly. Pump wormer
into the tube, warm water, and air. I
hold the twitch, while Doc tells his fingers, red from the
    cold
and white from the wormer, that horses
bring out the steel in women.

2

Chili and coffee at The Grill, and a walk through the Lower
Deer Creek Cemetery, granite table lamps, pink marble
urns, epitaphs with Old Testament first names, and bestial
    icons
get the Doc wondering if the Christians around here aren't
    a little
too much like the Egyptians and the Jews. He powders
their heads and tosses
testicles into a long glove that I hold open for our supper.
Horns and scrotums get lost in the straw, and barn cats
risk being trampled for a meal. Dr. Graves, after a twelve-
hour day, packing a testicle into a snowball that breaks
    against
the barn, tells me that the branches of a walnut tree in
    winter

are like the legs of a woman on a mattress of twigs, that
    dehorning
a bull sounds like cobs breaking. That he once
lay down with a woman under the axletree
of a cart just outside Lancaster, Pennsylvania, and when
we got home, if I would kindly peel the tunic
off the tripes, he could pour us a sly drink from the
    cider jug.

ROGER WEINGARTEN

The Broken Ground

The opening out and out,
body yielding body;
the breaking
through which the new
comes, perching
above its shadow
on the piling up
darkened broken old
husks of itself;
bud opening to flower
opening to fruit opening
to the sweet marrow
of the seed—
            taken
from what was, from
what could have been.
What is left
is what is.

WENDELL BERRY

Ornament

The children chased tumbleweeds,
blue variations over December snow.
Against the bunkhouse, buckaroos watched
drinking coffee splashed with Jack Daniels.
Steam drifted whiskey on the wind
as the rancher's kids hung silver bells on the thistles
filigreed with ice.

In summer the tin roof on a shack in Unionville
ripples like the snow peak three ranges east.
On the desert the calves are dragged & branded,
singed hide pungent as tarweed burning.
Ray & Dallas look for stragglers along the railway bed
leading to the old silver town.
Their horses' hooves uncover oyster shells
tossed from dining cars a century ago.
The hot air blows a ghost rattle through vetch pods.
Then out of dust whirling counter-sunwise, a tumbleweed
& the broken clink of silver ornament,
illusive & desirable, turns
through sage across the white flats.

GARY SHORT

Passing an Orchard by Train

Grass high under apple trees.
The bark of the trees rough and sexual,
the grass growing heavy and uneven.

We cannot bear disaster, like
the rocks—
swaying nakedly
in open fields.

One slight bruise and we die!
I know no one on this train.
A man comes walking down the aisle.
I want to tell him
that I forgive him, that I want him
to forgive me.

ROBERT BLY

The Black Faced Sheep

Ruminant pillows! Gregarious soft boulders!

If one of you found a gap in a stone wall,
the rest of you—rams, ewes, bucks, wethers, lambs;
mothers and daughters, old grandfather-father,
cousins and aunts, small bleating sons—
followed onward, stupid
as sheep, wherever
your leader's sheep-brain wandered to.

My grandfather spent all day searching the valley
and edges of Ragged Mountain,
calling "Ke-*day*!" as if he brought you salt,
"Ke-*day*! Ke-*day*!"
      *   *   *
When a bobcat gutted a lamb at the Keneston place
in the spring of eighteen-thirteen
a hundred and fifty frightened black faced sheep
lay in a stupor and died.
      *   *   *
When the shirt wore out, and darns in the woolen
shirt needed darning,
a woman in a white collar
cut the shirt into strips and braided it,
as she braided her hair every morning.

In a hundred years
the knees of her great-granddaughter
crawled on a rug made from the wool of sheep
whose bones were mud,

like the bones of the woman, who stares
from an oval in the parlor.

*   *   *

I forked the brambly hay down to you
in nineteen-fifty. I delved my hands deep
in the winter grass of your hair.

When the shearer cut to your nakedness in April
and you dropped black eyes in shame,
hiding in barnyard corners, unable to hide,
I brought grain to raise your spirits,
and ten thousand years
wound us through pasture and hayfield together,
threads of us woven
together, three hundred generations
from Africa's hills to New Hampshire's.

*   *   *

You were not shrewd like the pig.
You were not strong like the horse.
You were not brave like the rooster.

Yet none of the others looked like a lump of granite
that grew hair,
and none of the others
carried white fleece as soft as dandelion seed
around a black face,
and none of them sang such a flat and sociable song.

*   *   *

In November a bearded man, wearing a lambskin apron,
slaughtered an old sheep for mutton

and hung the carcass in north shade
and cut from the frozen sides all winter, to stew in a pot
on the fire that never went out.

      *   *   *

Now the black faced sheep have wandered and will not
    return,
though I search the valleys
and call "Ke-*day*" as if I brought them salt.

Now the railroad draws
a line of rust through the valley. Birch, pine, and maple
lean from cellarholes
and cover the dead pastures of Ragged Mountain
except where machines make snow
and cables pull money up hill, to slide back down.

      *   *   *

At South Danbury Church twelve of us sit—
cousins and aunts, sons—
where the great-grandfathers of the forty-acre farms
filled every pew.
I look out the window at summer places,
at Boston lawyers' houses
with swimming pools cunningly added to cowsheds,
and we read an old poem aloud, about Israel's sheep
—and I remember faces and wandering hearts,
dear lumps of wool—and we read

that the rich farmer, though he names his farm for himself,
takes nothing into his grave;
that even if people praise us, because we are successful,

we will go under the ground
to meet our ancestors collected there in the darkness;
that we are all of us sheep, and death is our shepherd,
and we die as the animals die.

DONALD HALL

The Tumbling of Worms

Back in the thirties, in the midst of the Depression, I
fled the city and moved to a Connecticut farm. It was the
period of my first marriage. We lived in an old gambrel
house, built about 1740, on top of a ridge called
Wormwood Hill. I had bought the house, together with
more than 100 acres of woodland and pasture, for $500
down. It had no electricity, no heat, no running water, and
it was in bad repair, but it was a great, beautiful house. I
spent most of three years, working with my hands, making
it habitable. At that time early American art and furniture
were practically being given away. Poor as we were, we
managed to fill the house with priceless stuff. We were so
far from the city and from all signs of progress that we
might as well have been living in another age.

One spring there appeared on the road, climbing up
the hill, a man in a patchwork suit, with a battered silk hat
on his head. His trousers and swallow-tail coat had been
mended so many times, with varicolored swatches, that
when he approached us, over the brow of the hill, he
looked like a crazy-quilt on stilts.

He was an itinerant tinker, dried-out and old, thin as a
scarecrow, with a high, cracked voice. He asked for pots
and pans to repair, scissors and knives to sharpen. In the
shade of the sugar maples, that a colonel in Washington's
army was said to have planted, he set up his shop and
silently went to work on the articles I handed to him.

When he was done, I offered him lunch in the kitchen.
He would not sit down to eat, but accepted some food in a
bag. "I have been here before," he said to me quietly. On
our way out, while we were standing in the front hall at
the foot of the staircase, he suddenly cried, "I hear the
worms tumbling in this house." "What do you mean?" I

asked. He did not answer, but cupped his hands over his eyes. I took it as a bad omen, a fateful prophecy, about my house, my marriage. And so it turned out to be.

Some time later I learned that my visitor was a legendary figure, known throughout the countryside as the Old Darned Man. He had been a brilliant divinity student at Yale, engaged to a childhood sweetheart, with the wedding set for the day after graduation. But on that very day, while he waited at the church, the news was brought to him that she had run off with his dearest friend. Ever since then he had been wandering distractedly from village to village in his wedding clothes.

As for the worms, they belonged to a forgotten page in local history. Late in the nineteenth century the housewives of the region, dreaming of a fortune to be made, had started a cottage industry in silkworm culture, importing the worms from China. The parlors of every farmhouse were lined with stacks of silkworm trays, in which the worms munched on mulberry leaves, making clicking and whispering noises. That was the sound heard in my hall.

It's a story without a happy ending. The worms died; the dreams of riches faded; abandoned plows rusted in the farmyards; one breathless summer day a black-funneled twister wheeled up Wormwood Hill from the stricken valley, dismantling my house, my barn, my grove of sugar maples; the face of my bride darkened and broke into a wild laughter; I never saw the Old Darned Man again.

STANLEY KUNITZ

End of Summer

An agitation of the air,
A perturbation of the light
Admonished me the unloved year
Would turn on its hinge that night.

I stood in the disenchanted field
Amid the stubble and the stones,
Amazed, while a small worm lisped to me
The song of my marrow-bones.

Blue poured into summer blue,
A hawk broke from his cloudless tower,
The roof of the silo blazed, and I knew
That part of my life was over.

Already the iron door of the north
Clangs open: birds, leaves, snows
Order their populations forth,
And a cruel wind blows.

STANLEY KUNITZ

The Farmer

In the still-blistering late afternoon,
like currying a horse the rake
circled the meadow, the cut grass ridging
behind it. This summer, if the weather held,
he'd risk a second harvest after years
of reinvesting, leaving fallow.
These fields were why he farmed—
he walked the fenceline like a man in love.
The animals were merely what he needed: cattle
and pigs; chickens for a while; a drayhorse,
saddle horses he was paid to pasture—
an endless stupid round
of animals, one of them always hungry, sick, lost,
calving or farrowing, or waiting slaughter.

When the field began dissolving in the dusk,
he carried feed down to the knoll,
its clump of pines, gate, trough, lick, chute
and two gray hives; leaned into the Jersey's side
as the galvanized bucket filled with milk;
released the cow and turned to the bees.
He'd taken honey before without protection.
This time, they could smell something
in his sweat—fatigue? impatience,
although he was a stubborn, patient man?
Suddenly, like flame, they were swarming over him.
He rolled in the dirt, manure and stiff hoof-prints,
started back up the path, rolled in the fresh hay—
refused to run, which would have pumped
the venom through him faster—passed the oaks
at the yard's edge, rolled in the yard, reached

the kitchen, and when he tore off his clothes
crushed bees dropped from him like scabs.

For a week he lay in the darkened bedroom.
The doctor stopped by twice a day—
the hundred stings "enough to kill an ox,
enough to kill a younger man." What saved him
were the years of smaller doses—
like minor disappointments
instructive poison, something he could use.

ELLEN BRYANT VOIGT

Permissions

"Young Farm Woman Alone," "The Tenant Farmer," "The Country Midwife: A Day" from *Cruelty*, copyright 1989 by Ai. Reprinted with permission of Ai and Houghton Mifflin Company.

"Horses," "For the Hog Killing," "The Snake," "The Broken Ground," "Prayers and Sayings of the Mad Farmer" from *Collected Poems 1957–1982*, copyright 1985 by Wendell Berry. Reprinted with permission of Wendell Berry and North Point Press.

"Passing an Orchard by Train" from *This Tree Will Be Here for a Thousand Years*, copyright 1979 by Robert Bly. "Cornpicker Poem," "The Orchard Keeper" from *Selected Poems*, copyright 1977 by Robert Bly. Reprinted with permission of Robert Bly and Harper & Row, Publishers, Inc.

"The Bean Eaters" from *Blacks*, copyright 1987 by Gwendolyn Brooks. Reprinted with permission of Gwendolyn Brooks and the David Company.

"Emergency Haying" from *The Selected Poetry of Hayden Carruth*, copyright 1985 by Hayden Carruth. Reprinted with permission of Hayden Carruth and New Directions Publishing Corporation.

"Roots," "To Ms. Ann," and "I Once Knew a Man" from *Good Woman: Poems and a Memoir 1969–*

1980, copyright 1987 by Lucille Clifton. Reprinted with permission of Lucille Clifton and BOA Editions, Ltd.

"Grandfather," "Gretel," "Gretel (II)" by Tom Crawford. Reprinted with permission of the author.

"Trees and Cattle," "Fence Wire," "The Sheep Child" from *Poems 1957–1967*, copyright 1960, 1962, and 1966 by James Dickey. Reprinted with permission of James Dickey and the University Press of New England.

"Farmer's Daughter" from *Tickets for a Prayer Wheel*, copyright 1974 by Annie Dillard. Reprinted with permission of Annie Dillard and the University of Missouri Press.

"A Sheeprancher Named John" and "The Orchard" from *To Touch the Water*, copyright 1981 by Gretel Ehrlich. Reprinted with permission of the author.

"The Black Faced Sheep," "Maple Syrup," "Names of Horses" from *Old and New Poems*, copyright 1990 by Donald Hall. Reprinted with permission of Donald Hall and Houghton Mifflin Company.

"Blackberry Light" from *The Chestnut Rain*, copyright 1986 by William Heyen. Reprinted with permission of William Heyen and Random House, Inc.

177